Mind over Body

*The development of the dancer
– the role of the teacher*

Maria Fay

Edited by Charles Hedges

A & C Black • L

First published 1997
by A & C Black (Publishers) Limited
35 Bedford Row, London WC1R 4JH
ISBN 0-7136-4715-9

A CIP catalogue record for this book
is available from the British Library.

Typeset in 10 on 11½pt Sabon

Printed in Great Britain
by Biddles Ltd, Guildford, Surrey

Contents

Part 4 THE ART OF TEACHING

Part 5 PRECONCEPTIONS

Part 6 THE TRIANGLE

Part 7 A REVALUATION OF DANCE AS AN ART

Preface

The procedures of studying and teaching dance were hardly ever discussed in the past though they are extremely important. They strongly affect the emotional and mental development of the majority of amateur and vocational dance students and young professionals all over the 'dancing world'.

In spite of the interest aroused by a few lectures I have given at some professional forums and by articles I have written about these matters published in The Dancing Times between 1992 and 1996, they are still not dealt with openly enough or with sufficient emphasis. This situation gives cause for serious concern since these are exactly the issues which influence a youngster's developing character and the maturation of personality, as well as the shaping of taste and responsiveness towards dancing and all other art forms in general.

Until recently, problems were more or less swept under the carpet instead of being openly and seriously researched, discussed or debated. It is no wonder that many well-meaning teachers, most professional dancers, students and their parents are unaware of the serious consequences which can result from disregarding these seemingly minor matters.

In writing this book I am trying to call attention to and to give some insight into these predicaments for the many people involved: dance teachers at all levels, school and company directors and dancers, parents of dance pupils, and first of all those thousands of students who are mature enough to follow and understand some of these problematic areas where they themselves could and should take the initiative to assist their own development.

However, for the majority of youngsters involved in the study of dance, training usually starts at an age when they may not yet be able to read, let alone make some sense of these delicate and complex problems! This book therefore also tries to serve as a guide for those who are most closely connected and interested in their progress – the parents.

Regardless of whether they think their children have any prospect as professionals, many parents give them an opportunity to learn dancing even when it requires some personal and financial sacrifice. They recognise the enjoyment of dance and the many other benefits which these studies may confer on their offspring's future life.

Learning to dance is indeed extremely valuable for every child because it is the only art where the physical, intellectual and emotional activities are entwined in perfect harmony within the training.

For parents who are not in the dance profession themselves there is scarcely any published information available about the complex nature of this art form or the many mental and emotional hazards which can arise during their children's long training. Often, parents do not appreciate the importance of a better understanding of the teacher's specific tasks and the many difficulties that need to be resolved in a dance class. This is even more true when a youngster has vocational potential.

Throughout the world, as far as most vocational schools are concerned, parents are uninformed and isolated when it comes to solving or making decisions about their children's occupational problems. Because of the parents' relative 'ignorance' concerning vocational matters there is neither enough liaison between teacher and parent, nor between student and parent. Parents lack the required knowledge because they are kept at bay, often treated as strangers who are incapable of understanding a dancer's unusual life and its unique circumstances. This seems to be entirely wrong and it should be replaced by intelligent communication.

Parents should know more about the intricate issues which concern their offspring's development as individuals without becoming possessive or dominant, and regardless of whether their children are amateur or vocational students. Apart from offering their love, parents should have knowledge and understanding of the issues their children may encounter. This will enable them to have patience and give sensible help and wise support to their children – and their teachers, too!

I hope this book will serve this goal, so I dedicate it to teachers, dancers, students and – last but not least – to devoted parents.

Maria Fay
Highgate, London, 1997

Acknowledgements

I would like first to pay homage to all those teachers who have taught me not only to dance but have guided me during my teacher training years to recognise in the art of teaching that **how?**, **why?** and **to whom** one conveys the subject matter is just as important as having a perfect knowledge of the syllabi. My contemporary teacher, Lilli Kallai, was particularly influential. Some precious seed must have been implanted in my mind which, during my entire life as a professional, has obliged me to pay great attention to certain specific values in the art of dance and its teaching: to the sensitive balance between physical, mental and emotional development and well being of vocational and amateur students as well as professional dancers and, consequently, to the way this can influence the progress of our art in general. I could never have written *Mind over Body* without having the good fortune of experiencing the beneficial results of some exemplary teaching attitudes.

I am much indebted to Mary Clarke who, during the past five years has given me the opportunity to express my ideas in the pages of *The Dancing Times* and who encouraged me further to publish them in a book. I received a lot of invaluable help and feedback from the letters received from readers of that magazine.

Special thanks are due to Patricia Daly who, from the time when she read my first manuscripts, asserted her faith in my abilities as a 'writer' and urged me to make my ideas known to the public. I am also grateful to Giannandrea Poesio whose inexhaustible enthusiasm has helped to strengthen my belief in the importance of publishing my thoughts in book form.

Numerous suggestions on how to improve this publication have been given by one of my 'star' pupils and close friend, Josephine Jewkes, by Anne Watts, my editor at the publishers, A & C Black. and by my 'long-suffering' dear husband, Peter, whose patience and support have been endless. I thank them all.

My gratitude goes to all my many friends and colleagues who have encouraged me to write my articles for *The Dancing Times* and have asked me to deliver lectures about neglected problems. This compilation is the result of their support.

I feel immensely grateful to all the students, dancers and student teachers who have studied with me. Sometimes unwittingly but most of the time deliberately, they have shared with me their successes and satisfactions as well as their intimate feelings and enabled me to discover the causes of their despair, anxieties, *idée fix*ations and other mental and emotional complexes.

However, I owe my greatest debt to my friend and collaborator, Charles Hedges, who was the first to suggest I write a book about my thought-provoking ideas. He volunteered unselfishly to organise my 'Hungarian-English' way of writing into a coherent English script. Little did my poor, naïve friend know into what a long-lasting period of 'hard labour and slavery' he had let himself. But he has honoured his word to the end and – what's more – has encouraged me with unremitting zeal (and still continues doing so) to keep on with my writing. Without his devoted work *Mind over Body* would never be brought to publication.

PART 1

NOT TRAINING BUT TEACHING

———————— ❖ ————————

Dancing Should Be a Pleasure

Public perception of the dance teacher is often somewhat misleading. When we tell people we are dance teachers, ballet masters or choreographers, the reaction will be, 'Oh, you must be very fit,' or 'That's why you're in such good condition for your age.'

The world around us has an impression of our profession being of a totally physical nature, an attitude which is partly understandable since the instrument of our art form is the human body. Our role is to develop and conquer this instrument until we are able to perform a wide range of movements, from the simplest to the most complicated and demanding.

Yet this is only part of our task. If style, musicality, expressiveness – in other words, quality of movement – are not additionally present in our teaching, we lose sight of our goal. It is something of which every teacher of dancing – no matter what their speciality, or which training system they practise – is very much aware. After all, examiners, répétiteurs and choreographers are constantly telling teachers and dancers that technique should be considered only as a vehicle for expression.

Nevertheless, as one looks at classes, at all levels and in every part of the world, one must come to the conclusion that many participants are more concerned with what to do than how to dance it. The attention will be focused on the height of the jump, the extension of the leg or the number of *pirouettes*, while the quality of execution is taken for granted, neglected or even lost.

Whenever I talk about this problem, the answer of many teachers, dancers or students is, 'We do appreciate the importance of quality, but there is so much to learn in so little time. One can only hope to add the refinements at a later stage.' Although this sounds a reasonable argument, I have serious doubts about its validity. Dancing is an art and, as in all arts, quality and technique are inextricable. The simplest step, arm or head movement is just an element of the whole art, and each part of that whole must contain the twin components of quality and technique.

This should be our main objective, and there are many well-known ways to achieve it – good musical accompaniment, the teacher's artistic sensitivity or stage experience, taking students to performances, watching and analysing dance videos. . . However, perhaps more important than any of these, there is something else – the creation of an atmosphere of trust between student and teacher, and an active collaboration between students themselves in class.

The syllabi of all systems of teaching are constantly changing for the better as we learn more about the way the human body works. Dance equipment such as studio floors, temperature control, clothing and shoes have developed so much more than the great teachers of the past could have ever imagined. Other enormous changes have taken place since the beginning of the century when teaching ballet meant either training vocational students or professional dancers. With the appearance on stage of modern, contemporary, jazz and tap dancers in the 1920s and 1930s, the study of these new dance disciplines, at amateur and professional levels, also became popular.

As a result, there are today great numbers of both vocational and amateur pupils studying side by side in schools. Accordingly, we teachers have been compelled, over the years, to revise what we teach. However, have we also revised the way in which we teach? Of course we no longer use a stick in class. The last time I saw one used was by Hans Brenaa in Denmark in 1963, and that was only to beat the rhythm on the floor. But have we totally lost the mental attitude that once physically applied the stick to a dancer's body? Have we become more persuasive and less dictatorial in our teaching?

As a student in Hungary I had a wonderful contemporary teacher named Lili Kallai who objected violently to the concept of dancers being 'trained'. 'Only soldiers, policemen, circus acrobats and animals are trained,' she would say. 'We dance teachers are not trainers. We are teaching intelligent, sensitive human beings to enjoy dancing, and encouraging the gifted few to achieve a profes-sional level of technique through which they can express music, emotions, moods and ideas.'

These principles have guided my teaching all my life. I am therefore greatly surprised when I still hear teachers talking like drill sergeants to their pupils, 'Tired or not, you will do it again and again. In my time, we worked until we dropped,' or alternatively, 'Don't fuss, you must learn to work through aches and pains. It is how we all had to do it.' It is small wonder that staff meetings take the form of endless complaints about students' injuries and their insensitive, unmotivated work. On the one hand pupils are told that the teacher is the best judge of how much their bodies can take, and on the other they are accused of not using their brains and lacking motivation.

I was astonished to hear the director of a famous international ballet school telling the junior students, 'You are not here for your pleasure, you are here to work hard.'

Should students, especially juniors, feel that classes are hard work? Should dancers feel that they are just doing a job, or should dancing be a dancer's joy and an audience's pleasure?

The pianist Arthur Rubinstein once said that he never worked in his life. For him, practising was always a pleasure and, if it ever ceased to be so, he would simply stop playing to avoid injury or insensitive, mechanical performances. Concerts were always a joy, both to himself and his audiences.

Where students train in a pleasant and supportive atmosphere the number of injuries drops automatically because of a lack of tension and stress. Naturally, some pain and injury are unavoidable but should we really advise our students to work through pain? The medical profession believes that all work on stiff and aching muscles could cause damage, and that continued dancing, even with only a small injury, lengthens the time of healing, and can led to chronic troubles. Wouldn't it be better to trust our students, and let them miss a few exercises, perhaps a class or two, rather then see them missing classes for days, weeks or longer?

We should also ask ourselves if the student is to blame for the lack of motivation. Should it not be the teacher's duty, or rather privilege, to inspire and motivate students?

When Nureyev was asked what made Pushkin such a great teacher he answered, 'He made the enchaînements so attractive, one just felt one had to do them no matter how difficult.'

If the teacher can create such an inspiring atmosphere in the daily class, discipline becomes voluntary. The student's devotion will come from the almost irresistible interest in the subject, motivated by the teacher's technically, and artistically challenging class.

❖

Skeletons in the Cupboard

Understanding dancers' adolescent problems

It is wonderful how today a variety of medical advisers are helping the dance teaching profession to bring up a new generation of dancers with much healthier bodies. Students in many teacher-training courses are learning anatomy and, in lectures, magazine articles and books, we are constantly reminded how, through daily classes, one can shape muscles and avoid injuries – or cause them. There is a big choice of remedial exercises to assist a dancer after an illness, accident or operation. These are often discussed in the open. However, very little is spoken or taught about how a teacher's attitude can help, or damage, the mentality of a future artist.

Is this because dance teachers don't care? I don't think so. Is this, perhaps, a skeleton in the cupboard? Maybe. Or is this important question neglected because, as so often in our profession, we are too busy training the dancer's body, and keep forgetting about his or her mind?

When we come up against such traumatic problems as anorexia, nervous breakdown, drug taking, etc., we generally cannot be blamed for causing them but we can't help asking ourselves, 'Could we have prevented them?' Perhaps we should have noticed the early warning signs, or taken more interest in the dancer's physical and mental stress at the time. I'm sure that most of us do think about this when tragedy strikes but we are inclined to stick this skeleton back into the cupboard whence it came. Perhaps we could pay more attention as to how our teaching attitudes can influence our students' mentality.

Not that a dance pupil's mind is so different from that of other art students or other youngsters. The basic aim for all teachers who work with children and adolescents must be that their pupils achieve the best standard in their subject matter while finding their own identity and developing self-confidence.

To help girls and boys through puberty is equally difficult for parents and teachers whatever the youngsters' interest is. But, as in most cases, it is even harder to cope with the so-called artistic or over-sensitive temperament. All kinds of vocational art school students belong to this category. But there is somehow a very important circumstantial difference which usually makes young dancers even more vulnerable than other art students. They need more patience, awareness and understanding, as well as tactful handling, from teachers.

To find out what differentiates a young dancer from any other arts student we have to remind ourselves of the often-mentioned circumstance that the instrument of our art form is our own body. We not only have to learn to play on this complicated instrument but we also have to shape and change it. It is as if a pianist needs to alter the configuration of the piano upon which he or she will play. Our situation becomes even more complicated because it isn't enough for us to make the body strong; we must, at the same time, finely tune it to perform innumerable complex movements which are totally alien for most human beings.

Athletes, acrobats and gymnasts have to do the same thing though in most cases their movement vocabulary is much more limited. Naturally, the preparation of their bodies can be more restricted. In a dancer's case immense care must be taken. Besides achieving muscular strength, flexibility and stamina, the body, or in other words the instrument, should be transformed and sculpted into a very specific object of beauty.

To learn technical tasks, such as turns and *adage* movements where the balance line is difficult for everyone, is tricky, but for the adolescent dancer it can become a nightmare. Just when the whole body is undergoing tremendous changes – visible and invisible – a dance student has to learn how to perform on a very unreliable instrument which is constantly changing in height, weight and proportion. The placement that has been achieved after a long and painstaking time, and which seems to be correct for certain technical tasks, cannot be maintained. It needs to be continually changed in order to follow the pupil's physical transformation. This may persist for several years.

Added to these factors is another more debilitating one: many youngsters, even if they never danced at all, feel tired and often suffer from growing pains in their legs. During puberty they may be prone to headaches, dizziness and other unpleasant period symptoms. Under these circumstances it can be very difficult for them to concentrate on any of their studies, whether academic or vocational. It is hard enough for a student to play a musical instrument, paint a picture or recite Shakespeare when feeling under the weather. Yet, the violin on which he or she plays is the same solid, unchanged instrument every day. Nor do the paintbrush, paint box, canvas or chisel change. But the adolescent dancer's instrument – the body – regularly plays unpredictable tricks for years.

We mustn't forget that in the case of some young dancers, especially girls, puberty can last for a very long period and, in many cases, it could be very belated. Because of the physical strain they are under, female students mostly have very irregular cycles and often none at all until they are twenty or twenty-one. This can result in excess weight. During these long years, dance students, and indeed even young professionals, are constantly battling with their own bodies. They find their instrument is letting them down, no matter how hard they are trying to achieve the required technical tasks. Aesthetically it can be very disappointing for them when looking in the mirror. They must see their inadequate or even disproportionate lines and often their ovate or overweight bodies. This frustration can be aggravated even more by having additional stress caused by participation in academic and professional examinations at the same time.

We dance teachers must also take into consideration that within the group of pupils that we are teaching regularly as a unit, the changes associated with adolescence are not generally synchronised but could happen at completely different times to each individual. The discomfort and frustration caused by these physical changes could take between three to six years and sometimes longer.

Let us remember that if any of the artist's tools of trade prove to be displeasing, damaged or unsuited, the artist can throw it away and get a better one. Dancers have no such option.

Just at the age when, for example, many young musicians are making a final choice of the instrument they most love and enjoy to play, teenage dancers may begin to hate their chosen instrument – the body. Ideally, this is the time when adolescents come to terms with and become proud of, and so finally love, their own bodies. All teenagers find this a difficult transition but for most dancers this is much more than a tough period of their youth. Being unhappy and ashamed of their physical appearance and frustrated by their unreliable performance, they will hate, and blame, their bodies. This hatred easily becomes the central force of their existence. They may feel that their bodies are the greatest obstacle to the realisation of their ambitions.

This turmoil and confusion can be very harmful to a young dancer's future if it is not channelled in time in the right direction. It is human nature that we become subconsciously angry and revengeful with everything that can become an obstacle to our advance. So do young dancers. They will want to penalise the body which they consider mechanically imperfect and aesthetically displeasing, but the instrument isn't detachable – they are stuck with it for life.

Wanting to punish their bodies could easily lead them on a very dangerous path. Coinciding with a natural ambition to perfect their technique they will start to work their bodies to a state of complete exhaustion, neglecting pain and injury. Dehydration and undernourishment are the next symptoms, rendering them even more vulnerable to injuries and health hazards. Luckily, some of these cases are detected and cured in time, but many are not.

This loss of confidence can lead to chronic or permanent injuries to both body and mind; quite a few react with apathy, end up with a nervous breakdown, turn to smoking, alcohol or drug abuse, or succumb to anorexia.

All these possibilities may seem alarming though they are not over-dramatised. We teachers must know about the dangers and need to deal with them. It is sad enough that in some cases we may lose talented young artists – occasionally the brightest and most diligent. But it is even more unfortunate when large numbers of students, who cannot be completely cured of these different problems – including anorexia – enter the profession each year, worldwide. Throughout their careers they will be unsettled, miserable and unreliable. What's more they will spread their unhappiness and cause many unnecessary problems within the companies for which they will be working.

It is a most disturbing fact that vocational dancing schools unavoidably become hothouses for these terrible problems. Experts are trying to help us prevent or decrease the number of nervous breakdowns and illnesses but there are no easy or safe solutions. In most cases the initial and main cause of these troubles is a loss of confidence. Therefore, creating the right atmosphere in our classes and giving our students every possible reassurance in themselves will noticeably help in its prevention.

Students need to feel that we believe in their abilities. By talking to them individually we must convince them that they can overcome their temporary difficulties. Once they understand that the problems are not unique but are part of a natural and normal process they will become more optimistic, more relaxed, and therefore more balanced in their thoughts. By good example we must teach them to be more patient.

In many vocational schools it is a normal practice to check the weight of teenage girls weekly. Teachers constantly comment on students being over- or under-weight. No doubt this is all done with the best of intentions but this only causes tension and aggravates the situation.

We must consider also whether teachers of younger age groups have a part to play in correcting these problems. Just as teaching fundamental techniques to young pupils vitally influences a dancer's further advancement in more complicated studies, building up a dance student's self-confidence, patience, and understanding about his or her body must be an important requisite in tuition from the very first lesson. At the other end of the scale it is just as important that teachers and répétiteurs in professional companies should become more aware that many of the young dancers who join their company might not have grown completely out of late puberty.

Naturally, it helps that some student teachers are studying psychology and teaching methods, but it is not enough. Open discussions and arguments by experienced teachers could give advice and warnings to younger teachers which would help them to apply teaching theory in practice. We could also think of, and assist, the many excellent members of our profession who have never received teacher training but who, after giving up a stage career, choose to continue their professional lives as teachers. Arranging lectures and discussions about these problems in refresher courses, meetings and congresses, and articles in the dance press, all would help them to become more aware and to understand the complexity and vital importance of this subject.

The greatest help we can, and should, give our students is to offer our trust, patience and love. If they are assured that we are confident and optimistic they will calm down and start to believe in themselves. If they know we can trust them they will not want to disappoint us. By achieving mutual trust, we can change a panic-stricken mood to a more hopeful atmosphere, lost confidence can be re-established and healthy creativity can emerge.

Let us take these skeletons out of the cupboard now and face up to them.

❖

Raised Hopes – Destroyed Dreams

Whichever their art form all true artists need diligence and total commitment. Dancers, however, need even more than that. Because of its physical nature dancing demands much sacrifice and self-denial besides dedication and perseverance. It is no exaggeration to say that, apart from talent, intelligence, physical capability and beauty, our profession calls for the devotion of a nun, the willpower of a mountaineer, the bodily strength of a lion, the endurance of a long-distance runner, the memory of an elephant, the industry of a bee and the discipline of a soldier.

The immense programme through which to achieve all this must be masterminded by the dance teacher; a great responsibility which should give us much to think about. We know well enough that even in the vocational schools only a small percentage of our students is endowed with all the above-mentioned assets. Even amongst those who do possess them there are probably just a few who have also that extra, and much-needed, dose of luck to enable them to fulfil all their hopes.

For teachers of vocational schools all over the world the first obligation should be towards the profession. Their role is to make sure that our art form receives on a regular basis a new generation of highly qualified dancers. But the same teachers must have consideration and compassion for those students – the majority – who by the end of their schooling cannot reach their goals. They have been nurtured for years with the same care and hopes and with a programme which, after all, has been tailored to the needs of an absolute minority. Even under the most careful circumstances, most of these pupils will be deeply hurt, probably mentally more than physically. The hopes and dreams with which they have lived for so many years are shattered. How can they not help feeling that they are failures?

I have often heard staff members at several different schools dismissing this sad fact by saying, 'Our students are warned constantly about professional hazards. We also prepare them to accept difficulties in finding jobs,' or 'It is bad luck indeed and we are very sorry for them but unfortunately that's life; after all they didn't waste their time during these years. They benefited from a good artistic education here and enjoyed dancing while they could,' and so on.

All this may be true but it doesn't alter a heartbreaking situation for students who wanted to be, but failed to become, dancers. If we think about these problems, we can't help wondering whether there is some way we can at least reduce the number of these psychological casualties.

We need to look at the early days in dance studies to try and discover where the roots of the problem lie. Thousands of dance schools around the world are teaching millions of children from a very tender age upwards, at an amateur level. This is wonderful for all concerned. Most children find dancing very enjoyable and it is beneficial for their bodies and minds. The dance profession will gain a great number of better educated, supportive and critical audience members; more importantly, these schools will provide the initial field for the selection of a new generation of dancers. Amongst these numerous pupils there will always be a number who are gifted, though only a very few will meet all the requirements necessary to enter a vocational school, and even fewer have all the qualities which finally make a successful dancer. So far there is no harm done.

Complications arise only when all those children with widely different physical and artistic abilities are taught together. Some of the more enthusiastic and ambitious teachers might unintentionally raise false hopes and dreams in many unlikely candidates and their parents. It is understandable, when talented and physically capable children are mixed with non-gifted ones in a big class, that an eager teacher would wish to raise the standards of the majority to the higher level of the few. Such a challenge could become useful to everyone in the class. A real problem emerges only when the teacher, quite unaware of any possible consequences, keeps dropping hints which refer in some way or another to 'the profession'. How easy it is for a teacher to remark, 'Don't give up so easily, dancers need endurance and willpower,' or 'Pull up your tummy. A *ballerina* can't stand like that,' or 'You *must* practise more if *you want to be a dancer.*'

Though these and similar sentences may seem more stimulating than harmful, for many children they could become the beginning of a hopeless dream. Even on a small scale, being expected to try to behave and act like a future dancer might start young dance-loving pupils believing they are potential candidates. Add to this the excitement and sweet taste of a school performance – being on stage, wearing costumes and make-up, being applauded – and, perhaps, hearing their parents' well-meant but not-always-deserved praises and congratulations, the youngsters are tempted to keep hoping and dreaming.

The mystery and glamour of a stage career, the shining images of idolised dance stars, the 'bravo'-shouting audiences, the flower-throwing fans, these can easily turn the heads of young pupils, especially girls, and often raise the hopes of ambitious parents, too. Parents' dreams influence the child, and vice versa, so the vicious circle starts to turn. Therefore teachers of younger age groups must be very careful not to express themselves in a way that can be misunderstood. Talking and explaining things to children and parents right from the beginning will help a great deal and eliminate further misunderstandings. Millions of children learn to play music without ever dreaming of becoming professional musicians. It should be so in our profession too.

Even more precautions should be taken at further stages in dance education. Naturally, most of the vocational schools are very careful and selective, and rightly so, at the admittance auditions especially as far as medical examinations and physical structure are concerned. This way they try to eliminate disappointments in later years. At these schools the atmosphere is absolutely professional and the students are brought up accordingly. They learn how to stand up to all the demands required for becoming a dancer when they complete their studies. They must believe in themselves strongly and must feel that they are capable of achieving these goals. They are conditioned by those thoughts throughout their years of study.

Even under the best circumstances there will always be pupils who, for one reason or another, won't be able to reach graduation. No doubt, this must be heartbreaking for everyone concerned but it is still better that they should know the truth than that they and their parents live with false dreams for a few years more and then find out after graduation that they are unsuitable for this profession after all. This happens every year, too often, with too many students, in too many schools all over the globe.

There are numerous private dance schools which open their doors to many students, and amongst the promising youngsters there will be many who have little hope of reaching the required standards. On its own this would still do no harm, just the opposite. After all, why shouldn't many teenagers enjoy the benefit of surpassing their primary and elementary dance studies even if they will never become dancers? Besides, it has been shown often enough that with patient and careful teaching, and the unpredictable changes of adolescence, a few of the so-called 'ugly ducklings' are transformed into 'beautiful swans'.

A percentage of those students who cannot come up to the mark as dancers, could one day possibly make good use of their studies in some dance-related career or in another theatrical field. Most of the private vocational schools make these distinctions and possibilities clear in time but there are quite a few that fail to do so. This may result in great disappointment.

During their long years of study these students also learn to think, act and behave as dancers should. Teachers demand conduct from all their students as if they were all fledgling dancers. Just a few will be selected in time, but several unsuitable pupils will reach graduation. Only when finding jobs proves impossible will they, and their parents, realise that all their raised hopes were false.

In many of the old-established schools in Europe, which are closely connected with major companies, it has become a tradition that pupils appear regularly on stage throughout their student years. The company's repertoire will contain ballets in which there is often something simple and suitable for the younger pupils to do, while the graduates and aspirants can cover parts in the *corps de ballet* or, in very exceptional cases, even some suitable solo roles. Gaining stage experience while still studying is most beneficial for a young dancer's artistic maturation and it is essential for the efficient running of the company, too.

Recently, some private vocational schools have decided to provide their students with similar, or even more advantageous, experiences. Sparing no effort and financial involvement, they bravely fight against all odds to create their own small performing companies. In some cases the members of these ensembles are graduates of the school. Here, indeed, is an extremely good idea which serves almost as a post-graduate year. This arrangement gives young artists, whose dance education has been accomplished already, an invaluable experience and builds up their self-confidence before auditioning and joining professional companies.

The other excellent solution is when a tiny company is formed by a school which has, say, a maximum of six senior students. The greater part of the programme is specially choreographed for their abilities and the leading roles are performed by professionals involved with the school. Some pieces may be created by choreographically orientated members of the staff or fellow students. The roles are studied and performances shared by all graduates. This way, every student has an equal chance to gain coveted stage experience – after all this was why the performing group was created. By alternating regularly in the cast and having experienced professionals in the leading roles the youngsters will find that the physical and mental load is not too heavy. In addition, this kind of project has the extra advantage of providing opportunities for young choreographic talents.

Problems may arise when some schools don't follow these excellent ideas in a reasonable way. Making up the groups, sometimes by internal auditions, they select just a small number of pupils from the school's graduate class. Such a practice creates tension and harms the unity and harmony amongst graduate students. In the long run, the result is rather negative not only for those rejected, but also for the chosen members of the group.

For the former the message must be clear: in spite of being allowed to reach the school's top class the standard of their dancing is considered inadequate for participating in performances which are not even professional. Up to now they have been studying with their classmates on equal terms. Suddenly, only a few in the class are given the so-much-desired opportunity of performing, while the others are denied the possibility of widening their knowledge and testing their talent on stage – something for which they have striven all their young lives. Hope will turn into bitter disillusionment, healthy competition into sour jealousy, teamwork into envy-driven combat. The harm done to the rejected will have greater consequences. Their self-confidence will be shattered by the realisation that even their own teachers have a bad opinion of their present ability for stage work, and all this comes just a few months before embarking on their career. What chance would they stand in getting a job, in a world of tough competition?

The rejected will feel that they are failures and become bitter, timid and frightened. Only a few of them may survive this crisis. This is most regrettable because amongst them might be some of those rare talents well known to us as late developers. Experience has shown that we can all be wrong in our opinions, especially at this period of a student's development. By crushing their hopes with our judgement at a time when they are vulnerable and probably not mature enough for stage appearance, we may lose a few very gifted artists of the future.

We should also investigate whether the 'chosen ones' really are absolute winners. Depending on the frequency and number of performances, and the technical demands of the programme being performed, the physical and mental strain can cause more damage than benefit.

A small number of students may have to cope with evening-long performances (often on bad stages) – which can include demanding, famous solos, and may encompass many different dance styles – as well as dealing with continual quick changes of costume in often unsuitable and cold dressing rooms (if any at all). They may be expected to pack and unpack costumes and scenery before and after travelling to and from performances, put up with uncomfortable digs or late-night journeys home, and to do classes the following morning with a very tired body and mind. This is likely to provoke numerous injuries. Though they will gain stage experience, even those rare ones who survive these stressful circumstances without having major injuries will learn very little about the real need of a novice dancer's first year in any type of professional company.

In reality they will experience only how a small group of not quite first-class soloists battle against an often not-too-well-organised tour round the provinces under quite difficult conditions. Certainly they will learn discipline and the validity of the rule: *No matter what, the show must go on.* They will also have the great pleasure of performing challenging roles and their hopes for the future will rise. With hard work, of course, they will improve their durability and, being young, they will have lots of fun, too. Nonetheless, they will have little idea of what kind of discipline, patience and perseverance is required from a young dancer to fit, with humble dignity, into a professional ensemble.

As far as their future is concerned, the sad reality is that not many of these students will get a job. On the other hand, those few lucky ones who will succeed, might often find it disappointing. They will have to adjust themselves from being glamorous, amateur soloists to humble pea-in-a-pod group dancers. Having tried to fly before they could walk, even jogging or running will seem to them too slow and uninteresting. The result might be impatience, frustration and unhappiness.

A few questions must be asked. Who gains from this tremendous effort? Is it worthwhile? The very students for whose benefit so much is sacrificed have to find out that all their hopes are raised in vain. They are also injured in body and soul, their dreams and self-confidence are crushed, too.

It is amazing how easily a splendid idea, devised with the best of intentions but executed with some misconception, can lead us to cause unnecessary distress instead of serving a cause. It is an admirable sign in the teaching profession that so much goodwill, energy, time and money are spent by so many devoted teachers wanting to raise the standards as well as the number of people learning to dance. Teaching youngsters to enjoy and love our art form is a noble and worthy goal. Creating a reassuring atmosphere in our classes, helping pupils to discover their identity and to gain self-confidence, and giving them every possible opportunity to prove their talent and find fulfilment, are a teacher's beautiful task. But raising hopes is a tremendous responsibility and we should consider very carefully all the possible consequences of our enthusiasm.

If We'd Had Just Half as Much . . . !

Bitter attitudes – repressed envy

In my comings and goings to different companies and vocational schools as a guest teacher, I often find that students, as well as young professionals, are rather ignorant about dance history. They are particularly lacking in knowledge about that most exhilarating and revolutionary period of dance which took place in the first part of this century.

I also notice that wherever I am working – no matter in which country or with what organisation – teachers are repeating the same condemnations, 'What is wrong with this generation? They don't want to work hard. They don't want to know anything. They've got everything. *If we'd had just half as much in our time as they have now!* It's all handed to them on a silver plate. . . But can they appreciate it all? Never. Remember what we had to put up with? But we wanted to succeed and we did.'

Hearing these remarks I have mixed feelings. I must admit that there is some truth in these accusations – though it would be wrong to generalise. But they make me feel sad as they often carry a somewhat bitter undertone. It is obvious that these teachers are dedicated and compassionate professionals; otherwise, why all the fuss? But how can they possibly continue creating a good, positive and artistic atmosphere in their classes if they have such a bad opinion of their own pupils?

After such outbursts, to cheer ourselves up as well as to retrieve some willpower to continue with the difficult task, we usually indulge in some nostalgic storytelling.

How difficult the circumstances were in schools and companies and how one had to fight and struggle, are popular subjects. The list is long: how frightening and severe or ridiculously unpredictable some teachers and directors were, and how one had no rights to one's own opinion; how often one was unjustly and rudely treated; how one had to obey without question the often autocratic ballet masters and directors; how small and cold the studios (and stages) were; how the only available studio sometimes had to be shared between company classes, rehearsals and the school; how easy it was to be fined for such things as wearing laddered tights, or having an unsuitable hairstyle or outfit in class or rehearsal, and how difficult to pay the fine on the little money one was paid, if at all; there was no Equity contract, not even a union; rehearsals could be endless, until dancers dropped from exhaustion, or injury, and one was often thrown on stage without sufficient rehearsal time; you didn't even think that all of this could be different or better – you just did it, and loved it all.

There were, of course, many things in the good old days which were excellent, even better than today. There are still many of us who, either directly, or indirectly through our teachers, have taken part in an exciting, pioneering period when the doors opened for innumerable, new adventures, widening our horizons. A time when new creations were born in different, fresh, movement styles. The art of dance experienced an earthquake and most people in the profession felt its tremors. It brought about incredible changes which still influence our dance life today. As it always is in such circumstances, some things moved forward at a much faster rate than others, and for the better.

For example, the emergence of so many touring companies was an enormous step forward in gathering audiences round the world and a new challenge to choreographers, répétiteurs and designers. It changed fundamentally the dancers' perspective. An enriched repertoire offered greater opportunities for a much larger number of dancers to show their versatility and artistic maturity. Travelling itself served as a much needed stimulus and eye-opener – dancers had a chance to see and compare the different dance cultures of the globe. The new lifestyle of a smaller touring company, entirely different from that of a large stationary ensemble situated in an opera house, put much more physical and mental strain on the dancers.

The achievement of the touring companies meant that the art of dance became more popular and international than ever. More and more pioneering companies were born, representing several different and new performing styles. Furthermore, a growing number of music halls and variety theatres, as well as shows, films, musicals and reviews, used more dancers, so more professional engagements became available. Dance schools multiplied in number and in variety. Suddenly there was a glut of thousands of dancers trained in different dance forms and standards.

At the same time jobs were plenty but they were insecure and often short-lived; partly because of the inadequate financial background of these new ensembles, and partly because some jobs, by their nature, were only part-time. In these circumstances, it is understandable that the majority of dancers, led by a passion for dance and a fear of losing an engagement, had to put up with all kinds of hardship, maltreatment and often humiliation.

Certainly, today's dancers should learn from their teachers about the idealistic and heroic struggles of the past so they may appreciate all the better the achievements accomplished by previous generations. We should tell them experiences and anecdotes from our memories in just the same way as self-made parents tell their well-to-do children what it meant to be poor, how hard they had to work, and how they fought to provide a better life for their families. Most youngsters respond to these tales in a positive manner because a curiosity about their roots and family history is natural. Why, then, shouldn't young dancers who love their vocation have a similar reaction? The problem appears not so much to be with a so-called couldn't-care-less attitude but perhaps with the reluctance or modesty of teachers to talk about their experiences to their own pupils.

If our experiences, and those of our old teachers, are interesting enough for us to reminisce about in a loving fashion, why can't we raise the curiosity of a new generation by relating our historical background from time to time? Dance history teachers, and books, are very important and can be as interesting as, and more accurate than, anecdotes told by a teacher to a student, but they won't have the same impact.

In ordinary family life, children and grandchildren can learn from history books about the Second World War, but its horrors and heroics won't mean much more than any other horrible war – probably just a few more dates to memorise. But when they hear real-life experiences directly from their elders – of how they fought, suffered, feared and survived – they will appreciate more the easy lifestyle which they lead now amid plenty and in peace and freedom, and may also become interested in reading about and studying in detail the historical period in question.

So, without any extra effort, and just by letting family life take its natural course (with the younger generation listening to stories of its elders), we can get the right results – more factual knowledge, an awakening motivation and, finally, an appreciation of the present by learning about the past. It is evident that if all this works effectively in ordinary life surely it should do the same for us. Yet, often I'm told by some of my colleagues that this has been done, lavishly, but to no use, and that today's students are deaf to such stories and sometimes are even aggravated, reacting rudely and destructively.

I recall some of the expressions which teachers used, showing a kind of mentality which may have been the foundation of these conflicts. Some of their words still ring in my ears, 'You are trying to give them your soul, your knowledge, your love. They'll just selfishly take it, and give nothing in return. They'll only make use of you.' And then the other so-familiar sentence followed, '*If we'd had just half as much. . .*'

If we choose to become teachers we shouldn't resent that pupils take so much, just the opposite. After all, this is why we are here – to give whatever we have and to help whenever we can. If students make use of their teacher's knowledge and talent, so be it. That should be our professional fulfilment and it should give great satisfaction. We shouldn't expect anything more from them. It's enough. We shouldn't seek appreciation or adulation. If you follow the above principles you will find that, most of the time, you will get a lot of feedback, gratitude, and even love, but expecting it may cause the reverse.

What troubles me even more is hearing the famous cliché, the 'If we'd had. . .' sentence. To me these words raise a suspicion of bitterness and slight envy. Is it surprising that when they are telling stories about their past ups and downs to students and young professionals that they will detect these hidden emotions? Sensing that their own teachers, whom they should want to turn to for understanding and help, are motivated against them by a mixture of repressed, unfriendly, bitter and envious emotions, must have a confusing and unsettling effect on them. No wonder their reaction is negative, angry and sometimes destructive.

Students of today are not the cause of the hardships of previous generations nor of the well-being of their own. They cannot truly appreciate the enormous contrast between past circumstances and present conditions, and take for granted that which is provided for them. We are the ones who created the prelude to today's situation. Actually, we should be rather proud that conditions are so much better today than yesterday. But is it really so?

Since the last century our branch of the arts has advanced a great deal, but as far as dancers and teachers of the Western world are concerned there is a long way to go before we will receive from society the same respect and patronage as our siblings do. With the exception of a few privileged and internationally well-known stars, dancers are still subjected to humiliating treatment which no artist of any other art form would accept. Dance is still the Cinderella of the arts world and, I may humbly add, dance teachers are Cinderellas amongst Cinderellas.

It is our duty to remind young dancers of roots, but this should sound like an invitation for further progress and exploration without a grim-sounding undertone of needling or jealous condemnation. Rather, we should encourage them, everywhere in the world and in each type of professional engagement, to continue demanding and fighting for even better circumstances for themselves and for the next generation. Dancers should be given a well-deserved position of equality amongst their fellow artists.

Preparing for Independence

Enticing dancers to learn for themselves

A major aim for teachers in vocational schools and companies is to develop in young dancers an artistic sensitivity which is combined with a precise technique. We advise our students not to be content with the skills and knowledge they have learnt, and emphasise that practising hard every day of their dancing lives is not just for the maintenance of the technical standards acquired at school but also for a continued improvement. Though we know that no-one can achieve ultimate perfection, we teachers constantly urge our dancers to strive for this unattainable goal. Conditioning for this idea must start from an early age, but the thought by itself, without knowing how to go about it when the time comes, will be of little help.

After graduation, dancers very seldom receive in their daily classes the same attention and carefully analysed, personal corrections which they had during their student years. In company life the classes are usually shorter, and overcrowded. Corrections are more general and given in a very speedy shorthand manner, which takes for granted that everyone in the class knows what the corrections are about. In other areas of professional activity – various shows, musicals, pantomimes, films and television engagements – most of the time regular classes and warm-ups don't even exist. Often there are no suitable studios available where dancers can practise by themselves, and a chance to attend open classes is rare. Dancers know that, without a daily class, survival is unlikely so they will try to do their best, whether they know how to or not, by practising on their own. By doing this they might avoid injuries but trying to keep up to previous standards, let alone surpass them, is almost out of the question. So, whatever the situation, we should prepare young dancers to work correctly by themselves and become, to a certain degree, independent of us before leaving school. In reality, however, this is seldom the case.

In ordinary life many loving and caring parents are inclined to overprotect their children. The dance teacher often makes the same mistake. Naturally, we are all anxious that our students should receive the best possible tuition during the last years of study; therefore we prepare carefully structured classes catering for each student's need which challenge and stretch their capabilities. Constantly we give corrections and painstakingly analyse the faults of each individual. We often give advice about diet, smaller injuries, when, where and how to audition, and what kind of remedial exercises to do, and we cheer students up when they are depressed, or tell them off when they get big-headed or fall behind.

However, trying to solve all their problems, planning their future (some schools determine their graduates' first engagement) without involving fully the students, or giving them the chance to think for themselves, is undermining their independence rather than preparing for it. Requesting them only to be good pupils, work diligently in class and follow with confidence the teacher's advice, may bring good results at graduation but, have we given them everything they really need for their future? Will they leave school as independent, self-confident young people with personalities strong enough to face a professional dancer's life?

The transition from school to company should be easier for those dancers who are graduating straight into an ensemble to which their school is attached, as in most of these institutions the graduates often rehearse and perform with the company members during their student years. Teachers of the ensemble may often give classes in the school, so students are in familiar surroundings, they know everyone and are known themselves by the time they receive their contracts. Even so, many of these youngsters find that adjusting to an adult life is not an easy task.

Curiously enough, students who find engagements in the so-called 'commercial' field are better adjusted, though they may work in the roughest conditions. As a rule, dancers who choose this type of career have more extrovert and self-confident personalities. During their last years as students they may concentrate less on classical ballet studies and more on contemporary, jazz, character and, perhaps, tap classes. These subjects, by their very nature, help students to overcome their inhibitions, feel secure, and bring to the surface their individual identities. Teachers specialising in these forms of dance not only accept but expect individuality, self-confidence, and a strong stage presence. A possessive and over-protective attitude wouldn't have much effect on these pupils; if anything, that could bring about a rebellious response.

There are, however, many kinds of graduating students who will find the transition to a professional life very difficult indeed. They are mainly those studying in private and national vocational schools who eventually become members of ballet companies abroad, or those at a school attached to a company who, after graduation, join another entirely strange group. They were educated mainly to become classical dancers, but the unifying style of intensive classical ballet studies unavoidably suppresses individuality. When these dancers enter professional life their personalities are mostly under developed and they miss the guidance and protection afforded them by the school. Many of them are insecure, confused and utterly lost. They will feel depressed, perhaps ashamed that they cannot cope with the new circumstances.

Some of them become so shy and withdrawn that répétiteurs are reluctant to use them often in productions. The fact that they are rarely given the chance to perform makes them feel unwanted and they become even more depressed. Their class work will suffer and their technical standards will drop. A weakened physical condition can lead to injuries, rendering them unsuitable to be cast in any piece. This process of disintegration may become almost complete and many will find no way out of it. Some will be dismissed, others will seek refuge in a never-ending chain of psychosomatic illnesses. How sad, only a few months after they have left their teachers (who have urged them to strive and accomplish the ultimate in perfection), everything has gone down the drain. They can neither maintain a basic technical standard nor keep a job.

With good fortune some of these dancers may find a stimulus to make a comeback and will start to work in overdrive. Unless they know how to exercise properly and how to correct themselves such efforts could become self-destructive. In some lucky cases, teachers, or older members of the company, may take pity and will help them to survive with advice and corrections. This will also allow the company's work to run a little more smoothly.

When we see so much talent and work wasted, we need to find a way to help these youngsters before they enter the profession. Companies have busy schedules and their work cannot be hampered by nursing the wounds of 'little lost lambs'. It is in the

vocational schools where students should be prepared for the
challenge of professional life. We teachers should not let students
do only the physical work, we should constantly make them aware
of *what?*, *how?* and *why?* they are doing that which we teach them
to do in daily classes. We should guide them from an early stage
not to rely entirely on a teacher's repetitive corrections but to
concentrate on their own faults and learn how to recognise,
analyse and correct them without outside help. We should teach
them how to warm up correctly and what amount of exercises,
and in which order, makes a good class. We have to explain the
importance of each individual basic exercise within a daily
practice, so that they will recognise how and when to make the
best use of them. We should also help them to understand the
application of remedial exercises and how to begin practising by
themselves after an illness or injury.

Finding time in our classes for all these points may seem to be
depriving our pupils of a few extra pirouettes or jumps, but only
by giving them this knowledge as well as good technique can they
attain independence. This is the way we need to prepare and arm
them for the long and difficult road ahead. They should be able to
achieve that goal which we set them – to strive for perfection –
successfully and independently. The dance profession needs good
dancers and mature personalities who have ambitions and are
capable of fulfilling them. To supply companies with such artists is
what good teaching is all about.

Practising one's own faults

At a teacher training course diploma party I encountered an ex-
student from whom I hadn't heard for several years. I learned that,
after a short-lasting teaching job, this graduate teacher unusually
joined a company as a dancer and that she was recently promoted
to junior soloist status. As we chatted, she asked me, 'Do you
remember when you made me cry at a teaching practice?'

'Oh dear, this is the kind of incident I would rather not be
reminded of. Why and how did I do that? What crimes had you
committed?'

'That's just it. I thought I was teaching brilliantly. I knew the
subject matter you taught us very well. You praised me for my
enchaînements and you found my demonstration precise and in
good style. You also appreciated my musicality and the way I

conducted my teaching. The trouble was that I couldn't recognise and then correct the students' faults in the manner you wanted us to. I was too busy teaching and doing the exercises with the students, so I hadn't enough eyes for them.'

'But that is the most typical mistake of a student teacher. I shouldn't have penalised you for that.'

'You didn't, you just made me watch the pupils dancing and then asked me to correct them. Though I could spot a few faults I still couldn't analyse them properly. I said a few things which I thought were clever but you pointed out that my corrections were vague and rather generalised remarks, not very helpful to the class. I became so unhappy that I just burst into tears.'

'Maybe I made a mistake in the way I corrected you or perhaps I was expecting too much, too soon.'

'Afterwards I understood that you wanted us to be better and quicker in spotting and diagnosing the faults as well as suggesting the right cure. I am glad now that you kept on insisting on this during our training because it is a great help in my present career.'

'How come? Are you teaching as well as dancing?'

'No. I am only dancing, but I meant it as a dancer. I find that professionals are compelled to work a lot on their own in order to progress. The shortage of time, and of good teachers and répétiteurs, allows little opportunity for well-guided practice or rehearsal. Mostly, they have to rely on themselves in order to achieve better technical standards and to practise new roles. However, if they work on their own without being able to analyse their shortcomings, they get overtired and frustrated and end up practising their own faults. Besides, if they are able to spot and diagnose faults they can offer help to partners and friends when seeing them struggling on their own. Of course, the ideal situation would be to receive corrections from a great teacher all the time, but that's rare isn't it? One can't have everything.'

This wasn't the first time that I have been made aware of the importance for dancers to receive the kind of tuition which enables them to analyse their own faults, or that teachers should be more pedantic about the way they correct.

When I was a student – like most of the other youngsters – I expected my teachers to be faultless. It was beyond doubt that they had a perfect knowledge of dancing and the talent to convey it to us in the best possible way. I took it for granted that their corrections were absolutely precise and valid, not only in my case but for my schoolmates also. If I couldn't get rid of a fault in my posture or master a technical task I was convinced, and mostly rightly so, that it was due to a temporary lack of understanding or physical ability on my side. It never occurred to me that a slower response to corrections might not necessarily have been just my fault.

It was only later, when I was working with a number of teachers and choreographers, that I began to notice how different my responses were to corrections coming from different personalities. I realised that the corrections I understood best and responded to most quickly sometimes came from tutors who were less successful with some of my colleagues, while often it was I who couldn't make much progress with some of those teachers who suited my friends. Sometimes this could have been a personality conflict, common in the theatrical world, but usually the real reason was that, though the corrections given by some teachers were generally valid, they were often made without proper consideration of the specific physical and mental make-up of the individual dancer.

Luckily, for every generation there are always a few outstanding masters who manage to get it right for the majority of their pupils. We all loved and respected them, and took for granted their exceptional talent to convey knowledge so well. Naively, we thought that the standard of these masters was the 'norm' and impatiently we dismissed all the others as inferiors.

This negative attitude shut our minds completely from trying to learn from them. The loss was ours. Perhaps these teachers and répétiteurs were not the best pedagogues but they all had considerable experience in the profession, sometimes with an outstanding dance career behind them from which all of us might have benefited considerably. Regrettably, the constant pressure in our profession, the fight for time and the impatient behaviour of youth resulted in a failure of communication between dancer and tutor. We wasted a lot of valuable opportunity, rehearsal time and energy.

Unless some dancers worked on their own in learning to analyse and correct their shortcomings, the situation could become pretty hopeless and depressing for teachers as well as dancers. These teachers felt frustrated because all their genuine efforts of help seemed in vain. It appeared to them that most dancers were inadequate, incapable, ungrateful, big-headed and unintelligent. Working under such circumstances created an atmosphere which was often paralysing and full of tension. Dancers had to make every effort to improve their techniques and, failing to overcome their shortcomings, they just kept practising their own faults over and over again, frantically.

Frequently witnessing such situations, I became aware of how privileged I was as a student in that I had some excellent teachers whose corrections I could easily understand, and also that several made me study in an analytical and self-correcting manner. At the time I was convinced that this kind of problem occurred only in my company and that the grass was greener elsewhere. Later, I learnt that this situation was prevalent in most companies, and in vocational schools, too. Sadly, it hasn't changed much.

One reason may be that many teachers believe – as I did for a long time – that to provide detailed movement analysis, and to enable students to make precise corrections and self-corrections, is important only at teacher training courses; dance students need to learn only how to dance and be taught how to exploit a brilliant technique. In their heavy schedule there is no time to teach them how to recognise and analyse their recurring faults. All this is the teacher's job and pupils should just follow their expert advice. If some correction is not understood that is due to the dancer's inability to comprehend. This seems to be a very convincing argument, but is it valid in every case?

The idea that analytical correction should be taught only at teacher training courses is quite justified, but in reality the majority of company teachers, choreographers and répétiteurs have never studied at a teacher training course. When teaching and correcting they rely on their own experiences and common sense; the one thing they will have in common with every dancer and teacher is that once they all received a dancer's training. If all dance education aimed to be much more analytical, precise and specific in corrections, emphasising and demanding constant self-corrections, dancers and their tutors might be able to minimise the frequent occurrence of these regressive situations.

Dancers . . . not Children

Treat dancers as adults

The lowly position of dancers in theatres all over the world was the subject of a conversation I once had with a famous ballerina. We came to the conclusion that, with a few exceptions, dancers are at the bottom of the theatrical hierarchy. No other artists are so little valued by managements, by other theatre artists or the greater part of the general public, excepting a limited number of dance lovers. The situation seems to be a vicious circle. In most opera houses dancers are given only a few performances apparently because they don't appeal to a wide-enough audience. But how can dancers give technically brilliant and artistically mature performances, and thereby win more public interest, if they have so few opportunities for performance? Interpretative artists thrive on the frequency of their appearances on stage but, no matter how talented and skilled they may be, without having enough stage experience they are bound to appear uncertain, nervous, unreliable and immature.

As we conversed I mentioned that I had tried to change the situation many times while guest teaching with various companies: writing petitions and suggestions, having endless meetings with opera house management, union leaders, directors, dancers' representatives and so on. But I achieved little except banging my head against brick walls.

'So did I when I tried. You can't do these things alone,' said the ballerina. 'I believe that matters will not change for the better until the dancers' attitudes change. They must grow up, stand up for themselves and expose their problems. Dancers have to fight for their art – for more performances, more stage and orchestra rehearsals, more involved conductors and so forth. They should demand these things to improve their artistic standards. This is how other performing artists such as musicians, singers and actors already do, but dancers don't. They leave everything to be decided for them, just like children.'

'But don't most artists have a streak of childishness?'

'Yes, but most dancers behave like frightened, indecisive and intimidated children. They don't dare to speak their minds, not even to their dance directors, répétiteurs, teachers and ballet masters, let alone theatre managements. They behave like children so they are treated as such.'

Every word she said sounded true; nevertheless, I felt that the picture she painted was incomplete. Dancers are often childish, but why? Could it be true also that if you are treated as a child you behave like one? Isn't it a fact that people brought up in an environment where they are constantly regarded as children, even when they are long past childhood, will naturally behave like children because they don't know how to act any differently? Besides, to remain a child may appear more convenient for many who lack self-confidence, and are not sufficiently prepared for adulthood; to face this can be difficult – making decisions, taking responsibilities, fighting for one's rights. These are tiresome and often dangerous and disappointing tasks which a child wouldn't be expected to handle. Who wouldn't try to avoid these adult duties, or at least procrastinate for as long as possible, especially if this were allowed and expected? This is exactly what happens to the majority of dance students and particularly to those who are educated in vocational schools attached to companies. This attitude persists throughout their professional career.

On one occasion when I was a guest teacher with an established company, I noticed that in the middle of my class one of the leading male dancers was excitedly giving a 'tutorial' about my *enchaîne-ments* to some of the younger members of the company. This was astonishing behaviour. I felt embarrassed about disciplining such a mature and internationally famous artist in public so I decided to talk this over with him in private but, before I could do anything, one of the older company members came up to me. 'Don't mind him, Madam, he doesn't do this out of disrespect. It's his way of showing he finds your class interesting and he's also trying to attract attention, something he's always done since he joined our school when he was eight. If he's naughty again, just tell him off, and. . .' Instead of finishing his sentence, with a wink he mimed, unmistakably, the action of spanking a child's bottom.

It was quite extraordinary, we were talking about a dancer of international reputation who was in his forties and a teacher in the company as well as at the ballet school. The director apologetically joined in the conversation, 'We are proud of our boys. They are very good dancers but I am afraid that they are a bit spoilt.' He used the word 'boys' quite naturally when he referred to about thirty-five to forty male dancers, the majority of whom were between the ages of twenty and thirty-six, with quite a few even older.

When teaching my first company class for another well-established European ballet company, I became aware of some giggling from time to time. When I questioned the reason for it the dancers apologised and explained that they found it very funny, unusual, but pleasing as well, that I addressed them in class as 'Ladies and gentlemen'. It took quite a while before I really understood the deeper meaning of this. These adult artists actually found it embarrassing to be treated as grown-ups.

I am ashamed to admit how often I must have been guilty of using the words 'girls' and 'boys' when talking to other teachers and choreographers about dancers who are, after all, grown-up fellow artists. How natural it seems to say, 'How did the girls do in tonight's performance?' or 'The boys are exhausted after these rehearsals,' and so on. This isn't splitting hairs about the accurate use of some words, nor advocating better manners in our teaching, but calling attention to the fact that there must be something utterly wrong in our own minds and in the way we relate towards dancers and, quite frankly, to ourselves.

Our unreasonable attitudes must affect dancers' behaviour. In turn this will influence the kind of image others may have about them, including their audiences. Perhaps this parent-and-child relationship is understandable in some of the traditional companies with attached schools, though it's not to be applauded. Members of the ensemble have usually joined their company's ballet school by the age of ten or eleven, and almost immediately start performing with the adults when the company's repertoire requires it. In these companies the atmosphere is very similar to that of a big family: parents and children, uncles and nieces, brothers, sisters, cousins and godchildren are often together in the same group. Ballet masters, directors and choreographers watch young pupils growing up into mature artists, but they still can't quite see them as adults, just as in ordinary life parents and grandparents sometimes can't come to terms with their offspring growing up. There are only a few companies with these family traditions yet, amazingly, in organisations where circumstances are completely different, people's attitudes towards dancers are just the same.

It is noticeable, for example, that in many opera houses when costume fittings are announced on the notice board the calls for the singers are for the 'ladies and gentlemen of the chorus' but for the dancers it is for 'girls and boys of the *corps*'. It's even more depressing when 'girls and boys' is used not just by the wardrobe department but by the stage management, administration and direction – a common practice in theatres where dancing is considered the least of artistic activities.

This expression, however, is used also in the so-called purpose-created, independent dance companies where, after all, the dancers are the most important artists of the organisation, and should be the most respected. It is even more worrying that the dancers themselves take this treatment for granted. They seem to find it natural that they are considered as non-adults.

When I was working in Canada with some independent companies, I found myself in some quite amusing and embarrassing situations when I heard people in authority, members of the public and even dancers using the word 'kids' all the time. At first I was confused and must have given wrong answers and mistaken advice before I distinguished when 'kids' referred to either school pupils, people's children or artists of the ensemble. Here it wasn't even 'girls' or boys', just 'kids'!

I thought this was just the American way of speaking until, one day, I met an orchestral conductor from the United States. While he talked about his orchestra it suddenly dawned on me that not once did he use the words 'kids' or 'girls and boys'; he mentioned 'musicians', players', 'members of the orchestra', 'soloists', 'performers' and 'artists'. As a matter of fact, I have never heard anywhere in the world an opera director refer to the singers he has engaged as 'boys' and 'girls', or theatre, film and television directors speak about their actors or designers as naughty or good 'kids'. Nor have I noticed composers suggesting they will spank musicians who have been a bit undisciplined during a rehearsal. Why then are these liberties practised in connection with dancers?

People often think of dancers as being beautifully shaped youngsters who are not quite ordinary people. Perhaps this is because the majority of dancers in classical ballets represent young peasants or courtiers, ageless fairies, supernatural creatures, and often the leading roles are of young lovers. Another reason is that dancers on the whole are fairly young people as, unfortunately, their active dancing career is limited to a short period of time. However, these reasons should not be an excuse for treating dancers as children. In ordinary life young people are not normally mistaken for children. There is even less reason for this to happen to people who are breadwinners, trusted with demanding, responsible and creative work. Because dancers' careers are so short we need to treat them as adults when they are teenage students so that their maturation as human beings and artists will be enhanced and might even happen at an earlier stage than that of most other young people.

Neither is it true any more that dancers, particularly artists of the corps de ballet, are all very young, nor do they always play youngsters or ageless creatures on the stage. What is true is that dancers are young when they enter a company's *corps de ballet* but only a handful of them will be promoted to soloist status after a couple of years and several will drop out for different reasons. The majority will stay there for their entire dancing life. If required, many members of the *corps*, at the age of (let's say) thirty-eight to forty, may have to play characters younger than themselves, just as the younger ones often have to perform middle-aged or elderly roles. Nowadays many soloists who are beyond their middle-forties still dance brilliantly and some of the character dancers give their best performances after reaching their fifties. Aren't we overlooking reality when we say that the majority of the dancers in a company are youngsters?

It is well known that the artistic standard of an orchestra depends on how responsible and mature the individual performance is of every player within the ensemble. The most memorable productions from an artistic point of view in opera, theatre, film, television and dance are the ones in which everyone, from chorus member to the leading role, gives a mature performance. This is even more true when performing the classics. The standards of dance production will also rise considerably if all the dancers involved are treated as mature individuals so they can perform as such.

Everyone agrees that children, if possible, should not be deprived of their happy and carefree childhood. Bringing them up, however, with an attitude which delays the growing-up process robs them of time to find an adult identity and form a character suited to an adult world. Life has proved over and over again that in crisis children can behave like responsible adults. Why then cannot, or will not, grown-up dancers act in the same way? It is because we teachers, directors and choreographers treat them as most of us were treated when we were dancers – as children!

While we try to do our best to ensure that our young pupils are not deprived of their enriching childhood, we must also watch our actions carefully so that in later years we don't rob our students and young dancers of that most important process of maturation – reaching adulthood.

Dance is the only art form where a mature and strong personality is required so early in life and, among artists, only the dancer needs to reach early maturity in order to fulfil a successful career. Let us treat them as adults.

❖

Workaholics

Common sense not overwork

I was rehearsing a difficult *pas de deux* with some young principal dancers. I had worked with the ballerina for several years but this was the first time I was coaching her partner. After hours of intensive work he remarked, 'All my life I've tried to work as hard as possible. The more I work the more I am pushed to work even harder. If, at the end of the day, I am not totally exhausted or in some pain I feel almost guilty. That's how I started out at today's rehearsal too, but I couldn't believe my ears when I heard your corrections – "Less force. More relaxed approach. Breath out. Take it for granted. Trust yourself!".'

Looking back on decades of work I must admit that I have spent much more time, energy and thought in trying to make dancers feel at ease in their practice and rehearsals, and in helping them to approach technical tasks with more confidence, than in doing anything else.

Working with professional classical dancers, one notices that the majority are, by choice, constantly overworking. What's more, while they are dancing and practising, they are using much more force than is really necessary. They have an almost permanently tense muscle tone. This can arise for both physical and psychological reasons, and it creates considerable trouble.

In the first place, using up a lot of energy makes muscles tire rapidly; continuing to work with fatigued muscles often leads to unsuccessful rehearsals and performances. Even if this doesn't result in injury it will make the dancer and répétiteur worried, so they will work even more, and harder. This, of course, demands even further power from an already-exhausted body.

Secondly, using extra force can itself be a reason to misjudge the precise execution of all kind of *pirouettes, tours-en-l'air*, turning leaps, lifts, etc. To correct these shortcomings dancers need to practise more – and more again. All these physical reasons sooner or later affect the dancer's psychological state; most of them will suffer from anxiety and insecurity. Though mentally and physically overworked they'll still keep on complaining about insufficient practice and rehearsal time.

The stage is set for all these artists to become 'workaholics'. Amongst those who don't belong in this category only a handful are, as they should be, healthily balanced and therefore easy to work with. The rest seem to be over-confident and big-headed. This narcissistic attitude is, most of the time, just a façade to protect a frightened, hurt and vulnerable person. Such dancers haven't even the strength of mind to admit openly that they have fears and doubts about their own true, or imagined, shortcomings and that they need help.

The truth is that most dancers feel insecure about their physical strength and stamina as well as their technique. This situation affects both the technical and the artistic standards of our profession. Instead of concentrating most of their energy on an artistic interpretation, artists who constantly try to overcome a fear of technical difficulties and an anxiety of running out of physical strength will never be able to give their dancing the magical and overwhelming effect that a good performance requires.

One would think that with experience, age and position in the company such a sense of insecurity would gradually diminish but, as a rule, the opposite is more the case. The higher the dancer's status the more technical the roles become. From the moment a high standard is achieved in a technically difficult role artists fear they will not be able to sustain the level they have set themselves and they might not be able to cope with healthy competition or to satisfy choreographer, director or public.

As if combating all these fears isn't enough, the biggest panic comes – always for the top-ranking dancers – when the roles are the most challenging in the repertoire. These artistically testing parts are usually the longest in duration and the principals may be on stage most of the time. They will have to dance in these works repeatedly, week in, week out. Leading dancers dread the thought that they might run out of stamina, and that they won't be able to sustain the impetus and hold together a full-length, demanding composition.

Working hard with such a troubled state of mind is an extra strain on over-used muscles. Sleepless nights follow exhausting days and often an undernourished and injured body will keep on working through sheer willpower. It is astonishing that dancers survive under these circumstances and hardly surprising if there is not enough time and energy left for artistic considerations. Problems undermine performances, leaving both dancers and audience frustrated.

Artists in other performing arts must go through similar problems but to a lesser extent. Actors, singers, puppeteers, musicians, mime artists, all strive for technical brilliance and, surely, need as much performing stamina as dancers. There are many who might be of the self-doubting type: a good sign of a conscientious and serious artist, as long as it isn't self-destructive. After reaching a relatively high technical standard at a fairly young age, particularly after achieving some individual status, an artist's main ambition will be on quality, whether in practice, rehearsal or even in performance itself. All fears and anxieties will be mainly about artistic interpretation, meaningful articulation, distinction in style, detailed refinement, doing justice to the author, fitting in to the requirements of a given production, and so on. These are the kind of worries which typically occupy the minds of interpretative artists and which add true dignity to their profession. Why is it then, that instead of being preoccupied with these normal problems, a dancer's concentration is to a great extent focused on failed technical abilities, and finding durability so as not to run out of steam?

Such concern is understandable for acrobats preparing for a show, athletes at a race, or boxers and wrestlers before a match, but it is somewhat undignified for an artist. Dancing is a very physical art form, and the greater part of looking after one's body condition should be done during student years and, later, in professional daily classes. Dancers usually have about seven to nine years of study before becoming professionals. Normally, they will spend two to four years in the *corps* and perhaps dance a few smaller roles before becoming soloists. A few more years will pass by before promotion to senior artist or principal. The preparation time needed to reach a required technical standard is ample. The traditional system of promotion gives dancers enough time to build up a performing stamina gradually. So, is this neurotic panicking of so many dancers justified?

It often happens, especially when working on new creations, that choreographers choose some promising young dancers to perform as soloists, and sometimes in leading roles. Instead of panicking or shying away inexperienced dancers normally take it for granted that, being selected for such a task, they'll be able to do it well and, most of the time, they do.

Success is almost inevitable. The fact that one is chosen for the task must be a boost to self-confidence and morale. In addition rehearsals will be reassuring as the choreographer will patiently give every possible help, encouragement and time to their own protégés. Artistic interpretation shouldn't cause any problems either in such an atmosphere; a role is made to measure and should fit like a glove, after all, that's why a particular person was selected to dance it. In such ideal situations dancers are less vulnerable to injuries, so the novice will sail triumphantly through this first big role as though in a dream. Unaware of any possible hurdles to be encountered these fortunate youngsters will have no inhibitions, no panic, no self-destructive doubts. The question is, what happens next?

A few of these successful protégés may be given other solo roles regularly, but these won't be made to measure and there will be much less time for preparation, probably hardly any at all. Working conditions will be more tense and full of pressure. Under these changed circumstances only a handful of these young talents will cope with the situation. The rest may suffer serious injury and could sink into a state of panic, which may remain with them for years to come. In these cases, of course, neurotic fear of a failure in technique and strength is understandable and might even be justifiable. In desperation the afflicted dancers can think of only one possible solution – to work more and more on their technique. Sadly, they will join the long lines of workaholics with little hope, unable to spare a thought for the intricacies of artistic interpretation.

After an early success, when a young dancer is selected for a specific leading role, it often happens that the newly confident youngster is returned to the *corps de ballet* for quite a while. Most of them can't appreciate that the management's decision is in their best interests and not because they are found hopeless. It is done because they are not yet suited to general soloist work and need time to gain more strength and maturity. After a dream-like success this re-grading makes them disappointed, unhappy and feeling inadequate. It is difficult to restore lost self-confidence and security even when months, or years, later they receive promotion. Facing the prospect of soloist work again after a long time suddenly becomes a frightening task. Self-doubt will lower morale in spite of the fact that they are about to achieve everything they have yearned for. One can hear them saying, 'I am amazed how I had the guts and strength to dance such a role in the past. If I had known then what I know now. . .' To overcome these doubts they will start working in a panic-stricken overdrive. In the long run early stardom and an unevenly developing career often take their toll. Instead of building up self-confidence, they may destroy it.

There are only a few artists with a special temperament who not only survive but actually need to be under pressure and stress to produce sensitive and meaningful portrayals. The majority will give tense and, with luck, technically competent performances but seldom exciting or satisfying or impregnated by their personality.

There are certain circumstances in a professional dancer's life which only choreographers and company directors could alter, but teachers working in companies and vocational schools could make a dancer's life much easier. In many case we could prevent them suffering unwarranted anxiety, overwork and their sad consequences. From the earliest years teachers shouldn't only point out in each exercise where the force should come from and how hard we must work to execute it correctly, and then take for granted that students will somehow instinctively find out how and when to rest. We must stress the importance of relaxation and explain clearly how, when and where it should be practised during a class, in an *enchaînement*, and even within one single step. Correct breathing needs to be analysed and constantly checked. Over-tense movements – not only the obviously grotesque ones – should be corrected just as thoroughly as too-relaxed ones.

Classes should be structured in such a way that dancers may learn the correct balance between tension and relaxation. Stamina will greatly improve if the best possible use is made of well-balanced muscle power rather than of undue force or sheer willpower. The aim is to achieve strength, stamina and skill with the least amount of effort. In this way practising technical tasks will become joyful. If dancers can take technique and durability for granted from their student years onwards they will feel secure and self-confident later on and fulfil all expectations.

We should make it absolutely clear to our pupils that though the answer to overcoming technical problems is usually to work on them, it is not the quantity of practice but the quality of it that counts. We should abandon completely the kind of teaching attitude which says, *Even if it doesn't work after trying it for a hundred times you must continue doing it until it does work.* Instead, we should prove to our students that practising a problem a few times with a thoughtfully analysed breathing action, an economical exchange between power and relaxation, and using rhythm and the right timing, must bring quicker and lasting results without slavedriving the body.

We should encourage dancers to work diligently but with intelligence. We shouldn't condition their minds to the misconception that overwork, injury and exhaustion are endemic to a dancer's life. We must nip this idea right in the bud. We should appreciate and praise those students who can find a way of using their muscles economically to produce their best results with effortless elegance and grace. We mustn't frighten them by telling them how difficult it is to master technical virtuosity. We should help them gain trust in their own strength, capability and talent.

By doing these things we can inoculate a new generation of dancers against one of the most destructive diseases in our profession – 'workaholism'. As a result both audience and dancers will enjoy technically brilliant and artistically inspiring performances.

Hurry, Hurry, Hurry

Racing against time

It is a characteristic of modern times that people rush through their lives as if their entire existence had just one meaning – to act, see, enjoy and achieve as much as they can in the shortest possible time. One obvious reason for this behaviour is that human life isn't long enough to experience all the things we would wish. We are racing endlessly with Time and, in spite of recognising that the obstacles are formidable, we still hope to succeed. This is certainly true of the dance profession.

There are very few vocations, and definitely none amongst other art forms, where the time element is so crucial as in the art of dance. A dancer's career is very short; a menacing thought which overshadows a dancer's life from the earliest days. No wonder both students and dancers feel that they must hurry in desperation. They are too young and too impatient to understand that Time, if challenged too much, can be a cunning and patient tactician just like a long-distance runner; the more we hurry the sooner we become exhausted and even injure ourselves. Either we have to drop out at an early stage of the race or, if the injury is not too serious, we may continue the struggle, but very, very slowly. When hurt and exhausted we can be nothing but losers.

Young dancers, however, feel that people in other professions do have at least a chance to make that long-distance run while they have only a short-range race. So they must fight Time with the greatest possible speed, hoping for the best. The race is on and before we know it we teachers become actively involved in this hazardous contest. According to our position in the profession many of us are often responsible for creating the rules by which it is played and judged; we create syllabi, examinations, competitions and auditions, all of which are meant to be hurdles or, in some cases, stepping stones. The great majority of teachers, however, are not involved in making these rules or in the judging of students, but the race atmosphere may affect their teaching attitudes considerably.

To do the work properly teachers in schools and companies would always prefer to have a little more time at hand than they actually have. During one class they would like just a few more minutes, but for a term they would want at least a few extra hours. Before examinations or a school performance, or after a whole school year, most teachers feel that they could use several more days, and after the whole period of schooling they would welcome an extra term to achieve a standard that is really satisfactory. So, teachers are pushing and students are trying.

Being a company ballet teacher is probably even more frustrating as there never seems to be enough time for teaching, coaching or rehearsing. Where a new creation is concerned a choreographer must usually fight a never-ending combat with time. The work's premiere always seems to happen much too soon, the result being that everyone in the theatre, particularly the dancer, is rushed.

These rushing phenomena also exist in the other performing arts and, indeed, in preparations for most other professions. The stress on the time element reflects on everyone's behaviour, but for dancers it is much more vital than for anyone else. In this vocation for every minute during the years of study and dancing each dancer must face the fact that at about the age of forty or so (and often it is much earlier) he or she will have to give up active dancing. At that age artists of other art forms are generally just starting to come to terms with their own identities within their chosen vocation. At an age when others start to mature, most dancers are left with only the memories of their dancing years.

There is a belief amongst dancers that if you haven't made it by the age of twenty-four you can forget stardom. If we agree that this is true it would mean that dancers must reach the status of at least soloist, if not principal dancer, and be at the peak of their abilities as well as mature by this much-too-early time of their life. What a ridiculous, impossible demand this is and what an extra stress it becomes on a young dancer's mind. Nevertheless, these are exactly the ideas which seem to become more and more fashionable since the occurrence of the 'baby ballerina' cult. Impresarios and others who were responsible for this phenomenon earlier this century justify its happening with the fact that in the history of dance there have always been a few teenage dancers whose extraordinary technique was matched with an early-maturing personality and so became the exception to the rule.

The majority of dancers reaching early stardom is frequently of the technical virtuoso type whose rise is due more to an outstanding physical ability than to a rare artistic quality. When dance students learn of the dazzling rise of such famous dancers they idolise them and wish to emulate these shining examples. So, full of great ambition, they start racing even if they are aware that most of these luminaries are, sadly, only short-lived meteors. Their exquisite shine may blind one for a while but mostly they disappear just as fast as they arrived. A disturbing factor is that these envied youngsters often become sacrificial lambs on the altars of commercial sensationalism. Sometimes they are even used for political and national prestige. Directors, choreographers and, especially, impresarios abuse these young virtuosi by overworking them before their personalities even start to mature. After a short period of heavy and stressful schedules a promising dancer's short-lived career may come to either a very sharp halt or often to an end, owing to injuries, nervous conditions or misshapen, over-developed muscles. What a tragic result for a young artist and what a waste for the profession as well as for our audience, to lose them – just for the sake of hurrying.

What a heavy price to pay, but still nothing seems to stop it. How many more young dancing talents will be lost from all those gifted students who will try but fail when following in these promising, over-rushed and risky footsteps? The saddest thought of all is that in this race with Time these casualties are still not the greatest loss for the future of our art form.

Students and teachers realise that, as a rule, the quickest way for a young dancer to achieve early recognition is by virtuosity so their concentration and ambition will be focused on sheer technique. Not only the body but the mind becomes conditioned to recognise and appreciate the art of dancing as nothing more than a highly sophisticated and stylised physical achievement of the human body. The importance of artistic quality is easily overlooked and forgotten. Rushing ahead, giving preference to physical performance and neglecting artistic values can easily become habitual. So, from an artistic point of view, a rather dangerous process starts to take place. Students become dancers who, later in their career, might become teachers, choreographers, répétiteurs, producers or directors. If the majority of these people in key positions give priority to technical achievement because they wish to attract audiences by astonishing them rather than touching their sensibilities, dancing might easily become a craft rather than an art.

This alarming process doesn't end here either. Dance audiences, like spectators of most other performing arts, are not a very homogenous group of people. There are several different reasons why people love our art. The physical beauty of a skilfully moving human body surrounded by the magic of the theatre always fascinates a great number of the public. There are many who love to watch the colourful and picturesque spectacle of lavish costumes and exciting *divertissements*. Others will prefer national and character dances, or fast-changing, geometrically symmetrical or asymmetrical floor patterns. Many will appreciate the intriguing rhythms which human movement can create. There is, however, another section of our audience, that of the real dance lover, which might enjoy all these elements of our art but which demands much more from us.

In the first decades of the twentieth century when the art of dance went through a phase of revolution an even larger number of people became interested in dance and started to find many different and meaningful values in performances. Choreographers gave more substance and depth to that which dancers could express besides physical beauty, and abstract works competed with fairytales. In the same way that dance makers influenced and educated their public's interest in the earlier part of our century, we help to mould the taste of audiences in our time. Dance technique has never been as advanced as it is today and if we keep over-emphasising this in performance we could lose the well-educated, deep-feeling, sensitive and critical part of our public. This would mean the loss of those very people whose sophisticated desires and demands motivate dancers to perform meaningful and artistic performances and choreographers to create imaginative works for contemporary audiences on new subjects, in new styles, which, from time to time, may give rise to masterpieces.

An artistically demanding audience is just as much a part of the process of bringing talent to the surface and creating masterpieces as the choreographer and interpreting artists are themselves. Dancers and dance makers whose minds are conditioned to over-taking Time, and to quickly achieving public fame and recognition by stressing virtuosity, might end up with spectators whose tastes and demands will be hardly different from fans of such activities as athletics or acrobatics. Their public feedback will be limited to their own technical skills and craftsmanship and will not enhance their artistic values to those who, given the time and opportunity, could and would become true, mature artists.

We teachers just might be in a strong enough position to help put an end to this process of decline before it is too late and yet another time-racing generation of dancers/dance makers grows up. We could turn the tide of this senseless, panicking haste by showing a good example – not rushing ourselves. Nor should we hurry our pupils towards premature examinations, competitions and auditions. We should not remind or frighten them about the shortage of time they have to succeed as students and, later, as dancers. We must exercise patience ourselves and show that patience is one of the greatest virtues which can achieve far more than frantic hurrying. Instead of the hysterical, racing spirit with which at present the profession confuses its youngsters, we should surround them with a reassuring, tranquil atmosphere where they can learn from us that instead of risking and neglecting their artistic values in order to beat the great enemy, Time, we could actually form a solid friendship with it and take what it has to offer for our benefit

> One learns with time.
> Time is a great healer.
> Time works wonders.
> Only time will tell.

Soon young dancers will be able to understand that we wish to teach them techniques which are not necessarily going to get them to their goal *faster* but which will guide them *safely* without great risk and, when the time is ripe, *will get them there*. This might also give more opportunity for their personalities to mature and for them to enjoy a longer and more successful career. Even if we cannot alter the fact that a human being is unable to beat Time, we may assure our students that they will have a more fulfilling, nobler, more enjoyable and longer lasting run alongside it. We, too, can be confident that if we succeed in turning our students' minds in the right direction a new generation of dance makers and audiences will enjoy again the emergence of great personalities amongst dancers, teachers and choreographers. These artists will lead us to the revitalisation of our beautiful art by continuing to create magical performances and new masterpieces.

To Show or Not to Show

*The question of demonstration – development of
personal style, not copying*

It has become a tradition in class that dance teachers demonstrate
the exercises, steps, movements, sequences and repertoire,
regardless of the style of dancing or the age group. To convey
technical and artistic knowledge to students by showing it to them
is the traditional method. As dancing is a visual art form this seems
natural.

Even a simple dance movement is a complex process which co-
ordinates a multitude of actions in a split second. To describe and
explain it in words can take a long time, while to show it takes no
more than the movement itself. The time taken to copy the movement depends on several factors such as its complexity, the pupil's
age, professional standard, rhythmicality, learning ability and
intelligence, but mainly on the student's visual memory. Even if we
take all these factors into consideration we'll find that as a rule to
copy a good demonstration is far easier, and therefore much
quicker, than to understand and perform the required movements
after a wordy description.

Therefore, if a teacher's aim is to achieve from everybody in
class the precision and unified style required for classical ballet or
national character studies the use of demonstration will be necessary. In teaching other styles where emphasis is placed more on
personality, spontaneity, imagination, expression and individual
interpretation, the need to show it repeatedly and exactly is much
less. This distinction didn't exist in the past. In previous centuries
the work of dance teachers was orientated in two directions only.
They taught social ballroom dancing and etiquette to amateurs,
and classical ballet with some national character dancing and
theatre mime to vocational students and professionals. As the
subject matter, goal, capability and social standing were entirely
different for these two kinds of students they were taught
separately and completely differently from one another. There
were, however, some similarities in the way they were taught.

The nature and function of social dancing in those times dictated that all the steps, movements, sequences and even floor patterns had to be executed more or less in the same way and style by everyone of social standing as most dances were performed in a group formation. For these pupils a busy social life didn't allow much time for dance lessons. Teachers had to achieve rapid results with a multitude of people of mixed talent and interest. Demonstration proved to be the quickest and most successful way; it was agreeable to the pupils and natural for the teacher.

During the same period in the theatres there were only classical ballet and stylised national character dancing. Great importance was given in most choreographies to the production of a unified *corps de ballet*. The aim was, and still is when these ballets are reproduced today, that all members of the corps should look and move in an identical manner. Naturally, to achieve this effect every dancer had to train in the same method and style for many years and from generation to generation. If an absolutely reliable notation system which could be read and understood easily by every student and dancer had existed for dance – it already did for musicians – the task would have been much easier, but it didn't, so teachers had no faster or more reliable a way to achieve good results than by demonstration followed by mimicry.

At that time all teachers in ballet schools and companies were active dancers or ex-performers. As dancing is not only a visual but a performing art as well it is understandable that when dancers teach they find that the most natural way to communicate with their pupils is to perform for them; besides technique, fine details in style and quality can be transmitted even to the youngest of students. As for the more senior pupils or young professionals, a practising artist's demonstration can be both encouraging and challenging. These are some of the reasons why, even today, classical ballet is taught with the same 'watch and copy' method, although nowadays professional dancers face very different demands.

Contemporary dance and jazz teachers don't only demonstrate but they often work out fully themselves while simultaneously conducting their classes. Besides the already-mentioned benefits the fact that the teacher is doing the class together with the students has an additional advantage. It transforms the daily practice into a kind of artistic workshop where students and teacher work together on more equal terms. Therefore these classes lose completely the atmosphere of drilling and training.

Instead of being a dominant commander the teacher has become an experienced, knowledgeable and spirited leader of an enthusiastic group of younger artists who are eager to study.

This ideal and gratifying attitude to teaching and workshop climate plus all the other so-far-mentioned positive factors seem to prove that the more dance teachers demonstrate the better the results they will get. If teachers involved with modern styles and ideas are also using this old traditional training method it must mean that it doesn't need any reappraisal. Or does it? Considering the enormously changed circumstances and demands from past centuries to this, and the next, can we be so sure that nothing in this teaching method could become out of date or negative?

In the past, if a few outstanding personalities arose out of a perfectly uniform corps de ballet, it was good enough. To become soloists these exceptionally talented dancers often had to be helped with additional coaching and master classes. In these lessons there was no need for any demonstration. The ballet master's job was to challenge and encourage an individual approach and interpretation. In contrast the majority of other dancers received tuition where the emphasis was very much on making 'peas in a pod', each one as equal as the next. Today there is still a similar need for both of these types of dancers regardless of the dance style in which they are engaged. How else could we reproduce the classical ballets of the past and how, indeed, could we create new works in both old and modern styles where not only the soloist but a strongly unified group is required? But if we examine this question more closely we might find that today in the two categories of dancers the proportions are changing. We seem to need more individuality than the uniform, 'one-of-the-same' type.

The subject and meaning of most new choreographies created for the large traditional companies seldom use the *corps* in just the old customary ways. Choreographers often want dancers in the group to move individually, to act and react separately. Sometimes they ask them to break away from the crowd, to show, as in real life, how changeable people can be and how each would react differently under the same circumstances. Nowadays, *corps de ballet* members should be able to portray all the various types of character within a crowd.

In contemporary dance companies, even in the larger ones, directors prefer to select their dancers for entirely different artistic qualities, looks and personalities. Choreographers find this a great asset when working on pieces which have no story line. These creations usually require a magical stage presence from the dancers and this must radiate through their movements. The more abstract the work, the more a performer's magnetism is needed to make contact with an audience and then to grip its emotions and intellect.

In musicals and other commercial dance activities, in addition to dancing, members of the chorus often have to act. Therefore, at their auditions, directors are looking for a strong stage presence and a capability for characterisation.

Besides the large companies and commercial theatres there are numerous smaller touring companies whose members cannot be divided specifically into group dancers and soloists. Most of the time each dancer does every type of role in turn but, unless all the artists possess a convincing individuality in this kind of small ensemble, it has no chance of creating anything memorable and will not survive.

Those twentieth-century inventions, television and video, as well as film, have a long way to go with regard to our art form; they are still at an experimental stage. Nevertheless, whatever has been achieved so far it is painfully obvious that the camera doesn't favour traditional productions with a large *corps de ballet*. These media, specially those using a small screen, by their very nature cannot allow one's vision to rest longer than a few seconds on a wide-angle shot of a whole stage with lots of people on it. Apart from the lack of definition, and the matchstick size of the dancers, the production would become boring if the camera lens didn't change frequently its angle of vision and focal length. The viewer is obliged to see smaller groups or selected individuals in close-up as the cameraman seeks either an interesting character or even just arm, head or foot movements. Therefore film and television choreographers will want to choose their dancers accordingly.

At every type of dance audition hundreds of dancers are turned away as unsuitable for the specific requirements of the directors, producers and choreographers who, in their never-ending quest for the right type, keep on complaining that they cannot find enough individuals who have that extra spark of talent – an explicit personality.

From this it is obvious that the profession nowadays is in need of many more different types of dancer than we teachers are capable of providing, and this demand could be even greater in the future. Of course talented dancers with good looks, beautiful bodies, satisfying technique and stage personality don't grow on trees but it is possible that even when there are some around we unwillingly might suppress, or at least slow down, the development of their individuality. It would be untrue to say that using demonstrations in teaching could be the only cause of an under-developed personality. We know that there are many other factors which may contribute to this. Nevertheless, it is important to consider this as one of the possible causes and, if it is, shouldn't we do something about it?

In my early teaching years, in spite of being warned by one of my favourite teachers, I didn't recognise the possible disadvantages of over-demonstration. One day I fell seriously ill and an excellent dancer took over my classes. After about two months I resumed my work and found that though my students had improved their technique their dancing style now resembled that of my deputy. Some of the mannerisms characteristic of this male dancer looked rather odd on my teenage girls. Interestingly, this mimicking of style was particularly evident in the more talented pupils – to pick up and mimic even small details in movement and its quality is part of being a gifted dancer. This experience made me reconsider the role of demonstration in the teaching process.

Dance teachers have various backgrounds as well as qualifications. They are of both sexes and of different ages, body proportions, body weight and so on, and will, therefore, have different dancing abilities. Some may be tall, others stocky, and some might have unusual proportions like short limbs with a long torso, or be heavily built. Many have a stage background but have retired through age or injury while others could be without any stage experience but perfectly healthy, perhaps young and fit but without a capability for turnout or extension. Some are more artistic and intuitive than others who may be methodical but don't have the gracefulness of a professional dancer. All these facts will influence their way of demonstrating.

Once, when invited to watch some junior classical ballet classes at a vocational school, I noticed that in one of the classes most of the children had an identical fault; when raising their arms to a fifth or even second position they lifted their shoulders as well. Though their enthusiastic teacher kept correcting this, the same fault occurred repeatedly. Then I realised that the teacher had an unusually short neck and short arms with quite prominent muscles over the shoulders and upper limbs. He demonstrated the *port de bras* faultlessly but the image created by his particular proportions and heavy muscle structure looked as if he was lifting his shoulders too. The children copied exactly what they saw.

Juniors will try to pick up whatever they are shown if teaching relies too much on demonstration whether it is beautiful and correct or slightly wrong like a sickled foot, arched back, rolling knees, mannered hands, strained fingers or floppy arms.

Obviously some demonstration is unavoidable, particularly when teaching youngsters and when we convey movements which are yet unknown to them. Even for the most senior students it is necessary when, for example, a specific style or interpretation has to be established in character and repertoire classes. It is very helpful, therefore, if teachers are capable of showing movements correctly when needed but it is undeniable that demonstrations may have a negative effect if not used sparingly. From a physical point of view it can result in incorrect lines, mannerisms and bad postures. These are common faults which are difficult and time-consuming to correct and most of them are also bound to cause injury sooner or later. The damage to the physical side alone is considerable but even more disturbing is the harm that over-demonstration can do, or rather not do, to the dancer's mind.

Some youngsters going through the turbulence of puberty often prefer to imitate the personality of somebody else – usually one whom they idolise. They like to shield themselves behind a mask instead of trying to find and face up to their own identity. So, copying a teacher who always demonstrates comes in very handy for the personality-seeking youngster. Wearing someone else's character seems a convenient solution to everybody concerned, at least temporarily, but not much thought is given to its long-term effect. If this hide-and-seek in puberty lasts a bit too long, by the time real personalities come to the fore it could be too late for them and for the profession. The loss is mutual.

There are other reasons why teachers should carefully weigh in the balance the amount of demonstration. As a young dancer I participated in a master class given by a world-famous guest teacher. He was still an active dancer and enthusiastically demonstrated and fully worked out every exercise with us simul-taneously. While watching the teacher's every move as we waited for our group's turn, a friend who always lacked self-confidence quietly remarked with genuine admiration, 'Isn't he just beautiful. Isn't he perfect. What am I doing in this profession? I'd better give up. I'll never be as good as that.' Overhearing this, another colleague, with a much more confident and rebellious personality, joined our whispering with somewhat less admiration, 'Neither will any of us unless, instead of demonstrating all the time, he'd watch us doing it and tell us how to do it better. Performing on stage he should be watched and admired; teaching in class he should be the one doing the watching.'

Though entirely different in their nature how negative were these valid reactions from very different dancers and how sadly disappointing this teacher's well-meaning efforts. He was far from being a frustrated-dancer type of pedagogue nor was he one who used teaching as an ego trip. He did't mean to show off, he was a real artist, but he made one simple mistake of which we dance teachers can all become guilty – overdoing the traditional method of teaching by trying to convey 'dance to dancers by dancing'.

In an interview the great orchestral conductor Sir Georg Solti spoke about his world-famous teachers – Béla Bartók, Zoltán Kodály, Leo Weiner and Ernő Dohnányi – with gratitude and reverence. Then he remarked that though Dohnányi was a first-class pianist and a wonderful musician he was an 'impossible' teacher. His idea of teaching was first to listen to his student's playing, with never a word of correction or praise, then he would play the piece in question without any explanation, just a demonstration of how it should sound.

No doubt Dohnányi took it for granted that the simplest, quickest and most natural way for one musician to communicate to another about music should be through demonstration, but in his teaching method – listen then play – he must have been mistaken if a student of Solti's calibre could admire him only for his wonderful playing but found that learning from him was impossible.

Dance teachers, also, should not be influenced by the fact that this way of teaching seems so natural, easy and fast, however beautifully the movements are shown. By using and developing the students' intuition, memory and imagination, we may easily do away with a lot of superfluous demonstration. This practice might be a bit more time consuming at the beginning but in the long run it should prove to be the right choice.

By reducing demonstration to a minimum the teacher might have to use more analysis of movement and pupils will have to concentrate more and discipline their minds to understanding movement analysis instead of employing thoughtless imitation. They will need to exercise their memories as well if they have to remember the style, rhythm, dynamics and movement sequences from their studies of previous days, or even weeks, instead of just being shown them over and over again. Movement analysis and good memory are essential requisites during a professional's life as self-correction and quick learning depend on these abilities.

We should also remember how much help we would gain in these matters if we could make full use of the accurate dance notation systems developed in the twentieth century. Hopefully, this immensely important codification will spread widely in the future, as did music notation. When every dance teacher and student can write and, particularly, read dance notation, over-demonstration and its physical and psychological harm will scarcely be a problem.

Finally, and most importantly, great consideration must be given to the possibility that too much demonstration can suffocate the personality of a budding artist and may hinder a flourishing perception, imagination and creativity. Deprived of these, future dancers and choreographers who have lost or borrowed their identities or who have no strongly defined personality, will never be able to contribute much to the progress of the art of dance. The question is not *to show or not to show?* but *how much?, when?* And *why?* to show. These should be considered and solved by all dance teachers individually and practised with great care according to situation and circumstance, bearing in mind the words of Oscar Wilde: 'Art only begins where Imitation ends' (*De Profundis*).

PART 2

RESPECT, TRUST AND LOVE

——————— ❖ ———————

Mutual Respect

I n an interview in Barbara Newman's book *Striking a Balance* (Limelight Editions, New York, 1992), Peter Martins, the famous Danish dancer and director of the New York City Ballet, says about his teacher Stanley Williams, 'He was really the one who injected the ballet in my blood, because he treated me in a certain way. When you're twelve or fourteen, you're not so worried about what you're being taught. You're more concerned at that age about, Do you like the teacher? Do you respond well to the teacher? Does he respond to you? Stanley Williams seemed to have a terrific aura around him and an enormous respect for his pupils. There was no looking down upon people or condescending. That didn't exist. Immediately he made me feel that he was saying, "This is a talent and I respect this talent." Of course, then you love him and then you want to work.' These few sentences touch issues which are of general importance to all teachers though Peter Martins is referring to his impressions at an age of puberty. A closer analysis of his recollections suggests that his remarks deserve serious attention independent of the age group of the students.

Amongst colleagues at vocational schools, companies or teacher training courses, we often hear complaints about young dancers who show a lack of respect towards teachers, pianists, or administrative staff and, indeed, towards older, experienced dancers and even disrespect for the standards and validity of traditions in our profession.

Such behaviour causes concern as it can undermine discipline in class as well as affect more essential issues. However, teachers should realise that a tendency to criticise established standards and authority could be a normal attitude of adolescents and we shouldn't over-react to such phenomena.

In all teacher-student relationships it is more important that we should re-examine and clarify the issue of the respect we should feel towards pupils and dancers – though many of us may think that there is nothing to discuss or that such a review could be inconvenient and counterproductive.

It has always been considered that a fundamental requirement – *condicio sine qua non* – for achieving good results in teaching is that pupils should trust and respect the teacher. Respect for one's elders is a moral principle of all major religions and philosophies. Even some revolutionary ideologies (with the exception of anarchical and nihilistic ones) hold up this basic law for both humanitarian and practical reasons. Without it throughout history young people would have become intolerant and life for a vulnerable and ageing population might well have become insufferable, giving full meaning to the words 'generation war'. Furthermore, in respecting one's elders one learns to appreciate the old customs, standards and traditions. The transmission of experience and knowledge from generation to generation was the cornerstone of human progress and civilisation and remains the unique ability of the human race. A recognition of past achievements is the foundation of present and future accomplishments which serves as an indispensable base for successful learning and advance.

One doesn't necessarily have to love one's tutors – though sometimes it helps to gain better results – but one definitely cannot learn anything of much value from people whom one doesn't appreciate, especially not in a physically and mentally demanding art form. Feeling respect towards one's elders and towards traditions is not only a moral and practical issue, it is also a precondition for progress. It is important that a teacher's personality, knowledge and behaviour should inspire such feelings. This is a very complex matter and to achieve it one has to approach it from different angles.

It is well known amongst teachers that the best way to arouse respect in pupils is by giving well-prepared, inspiring and challenging classes and also to become a good example to them from the point of view of discipline, professionalism and humane behaviour. There is no doubt these ideas are correct but they are incomplete.

'When you are twelve or fourteen' says Peter Martins, 'you're not so worried about what you're being taught.' Indeed, students at that age take it for granted that what teachers convey to them is correct. This is a good enough basis for students to gather adequate information and skill. However, youngsters at the age of puberty and with artistic temperaments might seek more than a reassuring thought that they are being taught the subject correctly. For many to make good progress they need unreserved trust in their capabilities, encouragement and constant confirmation of their talents from teachers whose knowledgeable judgement they trust and appreciate. If these youngsters feel they are respected by their tutors for what they are – namely, young, devoted and developing fellow artists who deserve good teaching, attention, care, love and patience – they will try hard to give of their best, just as the young Peter Martins did for Stanley Williams because, as he said, 'He had enormous respect for his pupils. Then you love him and then you want to work.' From these remarks we can see how much this respected student, in turn, honoured and loved his mentor. Clearly this relationship was based on mutual esteem so, as one would expect, the result proved to be excellent.

A natural part of human nature is that in certain relationships one individual's emotions are reciprocated by those of another just as the behaviour of one member of a human bond may provoke similar conduct from the other. From the beginning of time this fact was used, often subconsciously and sometimes knowingly, to bring about both positive and negative responses in every aspect of human life; in friendship, courtship, marriage, family life, education, business and politics.

Honoré de Balzac, a keen observer of human emotions and their reactions, wrote in his early masterpiece, *Eugénie Grandet*, 'Love kindles love'. This poetic aphorism is just as true and apposite as the reality of, let's say, 'aggression provokes aggression'. One might continue and conclude that 'trust stimulates trust' or, as in this case, 'respect reciprocates respect'.

Perhaps in no other human relationship should these mutual emotions have so much importance than in that between pupil and teacher, particularly when the subject matter taught is one of the arts, and especially when it is dancing. When teaching and learning dance, the majority of vitally important actions are motivated by senses, feelings and intuitions, therefore creativity and good standards mostly depend on emotionally highly-sensitive personalities on both sides of the class. In such an atmosphere it is evident that if receptive young dancers feel that their teachers respect them as worthy individuals as well as developing artists they will feel more confident in their own work and capabilities and will make better and faster progress. As a natural reaction, they will reciprocate their teacher's affection.

Numbers for Objects

The undesirable effects of auditions

Like it or not, participating in auditions, competitions and various examinations is an absolute necessity in the life of most interpretative artists. From a tender age they are frequently forced to attend to these stressful tasks to get a place at a vocational school, to apply for a scholarship or grant, to take part in various competitions, to obtain jobs and to gain promotion.

The importance of these trials has lately been recognised by most vocational schools as well as by the professional press. Dance students receive adequate information and practical advice on how to prepare themselves for these events: how to contact the organisers of competitions and auditions; where and what kind of companies have vacancies; what type of photos they need to send when applying; how to travel abroad and which accommodation to choose for the audition 'tour', as well as what kind of outfit is appropriate to wear when they present themselves at these functions.

Many teachers know the pitfalls and warn their students of possible unfair treatment, humiliating attitudes and other hardships to which they may be exposed. However, these warnings can only partly lessen the upset and psychological damage which many dancers will suffer.

In the world of contemporary dance, dancers generally are treated with due respect by their peers but, in most other fields of dance, competitions and audition practices give cause for great concern. This is particularly true for musical theatre, film and television. The mentality in which candidates are handled at the auditions of these organisations is often shocking. At these shameful 'cattle markets' in overcrowded studios, numerous dancers are labelled with numbers and lined up. If they are not already known to the director or choreographer, or their physical features don't appeal at first sight – even before they have been asked to execute any dance routine – they are often dismissed. One could hope that they be given a chance to show at least some of their skills and qualities before being sent packing. No young artist should ever be subjected to such treatment.

After attending a few such degrading and inartistic auditions as the above-mentioned example, most dancers with adequate self-esteem will find out quickly enough not to expect respectful and fair treatment at these kind of occasions. For a young dancer these are lessons of disillusionment and – though they may feel hurt, angry, cheated and disappointed – most of them will soon realise that, whatever the outcome, they must not take the results as artistically valid assessments of their professional talent.

By their shallow nature these infamous 'cattle markets' actually perpetrate less serious psychological harm than some of those auditions and assessments where everyone concerned is convinced that nothing else but an artistic point of view will prevail. The more superior the general standards at such situations the more seriously the candidates will take the outcome. Everything connected with these occasions, vitally important in their lives, will leave a deep impression and a long-lasting effect on the dancers.

There are some commonly used audition practices: participants dance in large groups; the audition lasts for only a short time; patronising or dictatorial language is used; and, mainly, dancers are obliged to wear numbers. These, at first glance, seem hardly demoralising. Even if some of the examiners and panel members realise that some of these practices are not satisfactory, they are scarcely aware of the hazards – by using these customs they un-wittingly may cause considerable psychological damage to the more vulnerable aspirants. The majority of them seem to reconcile themselves to these matters as being unchangeable: 'I honestly sympathise, this business of making dancers wear numbers is so dehumanising! I hated it when I was a dancer and had to wear them myself. . . but what else can we do to distinguish and select from **so many** of them in such a comparatively **short time?**'

Perhaps the answer is to change the habitual practice of exam-ining and auditioning dancers in a group!

It is unimaginable that students in other interpretative art forms – let alone adult artists – should be examined or auditioned in any other way than than individually. Why shouldn't dancers deserve similar respect? Isn't it amazing how we dancers first create these customs and attitudes and then put up with them though they are degrading and humiliating for both us and the art of dance?

In the professional operatic, choral and orchestra world, conductors and choir masters find the ways and means to give each candidate enough time, separately and thoroughly, while adjudicators of students of music, singing and acting follow suit. The question of 'how to distinguish' talented individuals doesn't even arise; it would be considered humiliating. These artists are assessed and selected from characteristics which make each an unique human being – their names, personal features, and their individual qualities. Is it only dancers who lack these distinctions?

Amongst all the young interpretative artists, only dancers in ballet and musical comedy are handled as if they were mindless, spiritless objects, samples of mass-production which must be 'tested' before being passed for use, and which – In order to be recognisable from each other – need to be labelled with numbers! Who wouldn't lose self-respect and self-confidence, when obliged to believe that one's personality is so insignificant that, without a number, it becomes indistinguishable from that of anyone else.

An ideal situation would be to assess dancers individually, at all ages and standards. One could argue that such an auditioning system might be more demanding, especially of the younger candidates. This should not be a deterrent but more of a stimulus. Students of all age groups as well as adult artists in the other performing arts take this procedure for granted because they are brought up to be self-confident individuals. Dancers, if treated with similar respect instead of being reduced to mindless objects, will also find this kind of challenge invigorating. Being assessed individually is dignified and the best preparation for acquiring confidence for performing and finding an artistic identity and stage personality.

Nevertheless, one must be realistic. For mainly financial reasons this is probably difficult to achieve in the short term but there is no earthly reason why the 'numbering' system should continue. Other methods should be found.

Already quite a few successful attempts have been made in the right direction, not only in the field of contemporary dance but also in the world of classical ballet. I have participated many times, both as a dancer and later as an adjudicator, at auditions where the panel would never dream of reducing the candidates to the level of objects. It might demand a little extra time and preparation from the staff in studying curriculum vitae and photographs of the entrants before the appropriate event, but it is worthwhile – nobody is numbered and nobody is hurt.

We should consider studying the better auditioning practices of our sibling art forms and adapting them to the specific needs of dance. By doing this we may well be able to prevent the next generations of dancers from being robbed of their human and artistic dignity as well as stopping the kind of treatment which can lead to the development of an inferiority complex.

Raising a dancer's self-confidence should be beneficial to the individual and will heighten inevitably the standards of our art form as well as society's respect for the art of dancing.

There are certain other aspects of the assessment procedure which could affect a dancer's mental development in an even more harmful manner than being 'numbered'. I believe these should be investigated carefully.

With the exception of some people holding auditions in the commercial dance world, most examiners on assessment panels are sincere in applying the basic requirements for treating candidates fairly and politely. Nonetheless, and in spite of much goodwill, events can take a wrong turn.

On one occasion a prestigious ballet company held an audition which I witnessed. After the artistic team had studied the curriculum vitae, references and photographs they had received, they selected over a hundred candidates to be invited for audition.

A few minutes before the beginning of the audition the schedule was announced: 'We'll divide you into four groups and each will be given a separate class. All of you will have to wear a number and you will have a chance to finish the *barre* exercises. Afterwards, we'll begin to weed you out gradually after each centre exercise. Those dancers in whom we lose interest will be asked to leave.'

This seemingly straightforward announcement brought a negative and discouraging element into the charged atmosphere – not exactly the ideal climate in which young dancers should begin such a challenging day! The healthy spirit of competition had suddenly been overtaken by the fear of being 'weeded out' and publicly humiliated. No sensitive artist can exhibit his/her best abilities in such a mental state.

Although the announcement of the day's proceedings was honest and all the teachers at the four classes behaved in a polite and affable manner – after each phase of the filtering procedure those who didn't come up to the expectations of the directorate were courteously asked to leave the studio and even thanked for their participation – the dancers' emotions still turned to disenchantment, frustration and anger. Why?

It was no secret that there were only a few vacancies in this company, thus it was no surprise that only a few candidates had any lucky chance of being accepted. Even if none obtained a job they were all looking forward to and prepared for a difficult, but fair, challenge. Instead, the majority of them were not even given the chance to get any further than warming themselves up with the *barre* exercises.

They felt – rightly so – there was absolutely no need for them to be deprived of the remainder of the class by being filtered out to such an extent that only a handful was allowed to finish. Their dismissal in public made them feel ashamed and hopeless. By no means was this justified: all exercises in the centre were executed in small groups and the studio was more than large enough to enable members of the panel to observe and assess every dancer's work.

The reason for the upset of these youngsters was in the **way** the audition was organised and the **way** they underwent frustrating and humiliating procedures, one after the other.

Only one dancer was offered a contract, although there were a few more places available. This outcome confirmed to the participants their conviction that they should have had more of a chance of working in the centre, allowing them to do *adage* and *allegro* work to show their technique and quality. This would have been a much fairer opportunity for their skills and artistic personalities to be on display and, perhaps, might have led to more of them filling some of those extra places.

It could be worthwhile to consider these dancers' arguments, and not just from their personal viewpoints. It is well known that quite a few ballet dancers may look somewhat insignificant at the *barre* but, as soon as they are in the centre to do the real dancing, they can offer a surprising virtuosity, quality of movement and presence.

At the audition described – sadly, not an exception but a world-wide prototype of a 'well organised' audition – if the invited candidates were not numbered and were allowed to complete the full class, if they were not filtered out in public, and if the choice of the best artists was made after the audition in confidence, none of these youngsters would have been hurt, their dignity could have been retained, and the company may well have gained several new talented members.

Fortunately, there are some company directors who are trying to find ways by which their auditions become valuable learning encounters instead of humiliating experiences for the dancers, and which will serve their company's interest as well.

One good solution is to invite a small group of dancers – whose work has been seen and liked by at least one member of the artistic directorate – to take a long and thorough class after which each of them is given a chance to dance a solo. The results (positive and negative) would then be notified to them in private by post.

Another much appreciated practice is to allow only one or two dancers at a time to take part on several successive days in the company's daily classes, where they will be watched and assessed by the directorate only after the last of these lessons. This system of auditioning is very beneficial to both sides concerned. Besides offering a chance to candidates to partake in several company classes, it gives them also a rare opportunity to gain an insight into the general atmosphere within the ensemble. By following a dancer's work over a few days the directorate will also have a fuller picture of that person's skills, qualities and personality (as well as shortcomings!) in order to decide whether they will fit into the company's artistic structure.

This seems a sensible and sensitive approach with no necessity for any of those frustrating and embarrassing situations where such a humiliating phrase as 'Weed YOU out' can be used. Compared to other issues this may seem only a small matter. Probably even the dancers are hardly aware of its poison as they have become used to hearing it during their school days at assessment classes, and other events.

'It isn't a very nice way to talk,' admitted a fellow adjudicator, when I mentioned my indignation about the use of the word 'weeding' in connection with any human being, 'but it's just a manner of speech, a rather thoughtless cliché.'

That may be so, but this 'rather thoughtless cliché' can deeply hurt many people. Doesn't this manner of speech express just the kind of attitude so typical of, and damaging to, our profession? Or is this just splitting hairs?

According to the *Oxford English Dictionary* the definition of a 'weed' is: 'Wild herb springing where it is **not wanted**' and in its verbal form: 'sort out (**inferior** parts or members of a quantity or company) for riddance'.

From this one audition alone more than a hundred young dancers (with one exception) were given the painful impression that they were unwanted, inferior, someone for riddance from the profession, in fact, just weeds! How many hundreds of others are being hurt regularly, audition by audition, year by year?

One might suggest it better to 'weed out' these thoughtless and insensitive clichés from our professional vocabulary and 'sort out for riddance' the wrong attitudes, instead of the young, vulnerable dancers from auditions and similar activities. For the future shouldn't we consider auditions as functions of selection which – according to the *OED* – means picking out the best, or **choosing for excellence.**

Come On, Bertha, Jump!

How to stimulate

I t was during my early teaching days that a particular vocational school graduate called into my studio. She lacked elevation and hoped to overcome the problem through some specific private lessons. Apart from this fault she was a talented dancer with a well-proportioned body, lovely extensions, beautiful feet – with which she worked with great precision – a fairly strong back and pleasing *port de bras*. Her Achilles tendon was no shorter than average so to try and solve her problem seemed an interesting and worthwhile challenge.

She was a student from abroad so I had little opportunity to learn much about her early training. I explained that her defect could have been caused by numerous physical or psychological reasons, and perhaps stemmed from previous or present practice. Therefore we might need time, patience and perseverance to detect and eventually overcome the cause.

'Oh, I don't think you have to worry too much about my past training from this point of view. Before I came to this country to study seriously and professionally I'd just about managed a satisfactory *ballon*. With vocational training I hoped to be able to improve it but, instead, I seem to have lost it as well as any confidence that I'll ever find it again.'

'Have you had any injury or illness since then?'

'Nothing at all. I'm much stronger than before and as far as my technique is concerned I've made good progress. Nevertheless, no-one here can make me jump so well as my teacher at home could. She helped me so much with this problem.'

'Ah, how?'

Waiting eagerly for the answer, I thought I was on the right track to find a clue in this mystery of lost elevation and hope. I expected to hear something about a special method, a different approach or some supplementary exercises. Perhaps this teacher used musical accents or time signatures to a better advantage, or was the secret of her success simply the way she linked jumps together in an *enchaînement*? Perhaps she structured her class differently while leading up to the *allegro* section or were her movement analyses and corrections so exceptionally clear? Could it be possible that the teacher abroad knew something special which we in England should have known, but didn't? Only curiosity was greater than my secret envy; I couldn't wait for the revelations.

My astonishment was even greater than my expectation when I heard the girl say: 'When we practised our *allegro* exercises my teacher kept on shouting at me with encouragement, "Come on, Bertha, jump" and she'd clap her hands and raise her arms and snap her fingers and stamp her foot with immense energy. She wanted me to jump so much that, I guess, I had to do it for her.'

Oh dear, is that it? So much for special methods, supplementary exercises, movement analysis, different musical accents, and all the other things that intelligent and well-qualified teachers believe in.

Of course, from the student's simple narrative I would never have found out how much of her story was truth and how much imagination but, though it sounded very naive, it disturbed me. I couldn't possibly take seriously her description but, at the same time, I also sensed that I shouldn't dismiss it entirely because somehow, somewhere, there might be a sensible message in it.

In my confusion my immediate reaction must have been quite sarcastic and snobbish, and rather embarrassing for her when I said, 'Is this what you expect me to do? I think I should tackle your problem more professionally and analytically to achieve a lasting result.'

At that stage in my career I might have had some knowledge about technique but certainly not enough experience in practical teaching to realise that mocking both teacher and anecdote was a mistake. Little did I know that later in life I would reappraise the situation very differently. I don't mean to say that today I agree with the way this teacher tried to make a basically *terre-à-terre* student jump better, that is if one considers that this is all she did, because I believe more than ever in the importance of a logical and methodical way of teaching. I am convinced that we can overcome some of the difficulties in our pupils' technique by systematically searching for the causes and, when we find them, explain the reasons and how to correct them. Indeed, all the animated 'come-on-Bertha-jump' encouragement in the whole world could not be the answer when the question 'HOW?' arises. However, I realise now that psychological factors influence the results of our teaching just as much as, and occasionally more than, physical conditions. There was much to conclude from this unpretentious story but even more to be learnt if one has the conviction that mental factors can markedly affect the physical output.

These facts are particularly noticeable when watching, for example, athletics, especially on those occasions when a record might be broken. Some of the athletes taking part in such competitive sports as the high jump, long jump, javelin and other individual games often signal to spectators to clap and cheer for them while they prepare themselves, and even during the event. Obviously they expect inspiration from the crowd's audible enthusiasm. They hope that the ardent atmosphere will help them reach a kind of ecstatic state which might result in some extraordinary physical achievement.

This ancient, almost primitive way of boosting morale works very well, most of the time, because it is pregnant with components that help humans excel their own physical limits. It seems very important to individuals to be reassured that they are not alone at a time when they need extra strength or stamina. This gives them confidence.

The thought that a great personal ambition is supported by others, not only as a result of human compassion but also because the cause itself seems to matter very much to them, makes them realise how significant their action must be. This fills them with noble pride.

In the spectators' stimulating cheers there is also a declaration of trust in the talent of the individual, to fulfil their great expectation. This trust might easily awaken a sense of responsibility, besides the self-confidence and pride, which says, 'I cannot let down these people who believe in me so much!' A person from whom so much is expected will make the greatest effort to please rather than disappoint.

All these external psychological stimuli, combined with internal rousing effects such as ambition and willpower, may result in a state of mind which can produce an extraordinary, almost superhuman, physical strength. Since the days of the original Olympic Games this has been taken for granted. Why shouldn't the same happen in young Bertha's case?

Her enthusiastic teacher acted the role of a cheering, compassionate and trusting crowd and, because of this, Bertha didn't feel alone in the process of mastering something which was difficult for her. She felt that she had the support, trust and expectation of the very person whom she believed to be the best judge of her capabilities. Also she must have felt that her teacher would be very disappointed if she couldn't come up to her expectations. Evidently, the simple but genuine and ancient method of morale-boosting worked as she tried even harder for her encouraging pedagogue – *and Bertha jumped!* But in the absence of her old mentor, Bertha couldn't do so well and even lost her confidence.

Naturally, one could never advocate a teaching method which achieved results based only on these ideas. Without using methods deriving from human anatomy and physiology, extraneous physical achievements might only be temporary and could also cause injuries.

However, a teacher's strong and positive personality can have an almost magical influence on the actions of dancers. For this one can hardly find a better example than that of the late Dame Marie Rambert. She was a life force within her company and seemed to have an almost magical influence on the dancers. During a performance she would stand in the wings and encourage them, much to the delight of a surprised audience. In the small Mercury Theatre they couldn't help but hear her loud, enhancing commentary and enjoyed it enormously, not only because they found this situation charming, funny and unusual, but also because they sometimes witnessed truly magical performances, induced by Madame's behaviour. As for the dancers, they openly admitted that they often excelled their usual technical standards because of 'Mim's shouting'.

Of course, enhancing our dancers' capabilities doesn't necessarily mean shouting, stamping and clapping. It may manifest itself in many different ways according to the teacher's and student's personalities, but the importance of constant support is indisputable. Great consideration must be given to how one successfully combines an atmosphere of trust, hope and excitement with logically structured, factual and corrective training. With the right mixture Bertha wouldn't have lost her elevation suddenly nor her hope that she could regain it.

---------------- ❖ ----------------

One to One

Individual coaching

When dancers become stuck over some specific technical hurdle, or struggle with recurring injuries or are in need of rehabilitation after illness, the root of their problems often turns out to be more of a psychological nature than a purely physical one and is usually a rather complex mixture of the two.

To find the often obscure physical causes of some faults can be a painstaking exercise. To seek the psychological origins at the same time may even be more trying and time-consuming. It is like attempting to complete a complicated jigsaw puzzle but the difference is that dealing with an artist's emotions, brain and body requires more than patience and a special gift for observation; tact and skill are needed as well. If the cause of the problem is purely physical, once it has been identified the dancer may correct it more easily and faster than if it has a deeply rooted psychological origin (perhaps from their early training period).

Though the ideal situation would be to investigate each dancer's specific problems from both angles, circumstances in a dance company seldom offer this opportunity. This is why so many professionals seek help in the form of private lessons outside their company's official schedule.

If problems stem from psychological causes, even if the dancers are unaware of them, it is quite usual for them to turn instinctively to a guest or freelance teacher unconnected with the company's staff who will deal with the problem in a private and discreet manner.

Generally, directors of dance companies, especially ballet ones, dislike this and often forbid these consultations. There are valid and understandable reasons for this prohibition. Each company attempts to achieve, and retain, a style of its own. The various outside teacher – who might have different styles and ideas – while working with individual dancers could unintentionally have a disturbing influence on an ensemble's unified style.

However, if taken at its face value, this theory is debatable.

Many times throughout ballet history it has been shown that these intimate private coaching sessions have often turned out to be very beneficial for the individual artist and generally reflected favourably on the company's work as a whole.

I have observed these arguments from both the 'inside' and 'outside' – as a dancer, then as a regular ballet mistress, and later as a guest or freelance teacher. I have often asked myself why dancers choose this arduous solution, whenever they have some technical 'hurdle' or, due to injury or illness, they require a rehabilitation period (and who hasn't suffered some of these during one's career?). It often means getting oneself into trouble and having to cope with additional work on top of an already heavy schedule. If dancers choose to work with a teacher outside their company – often the most favoured course – they also need to be prepared for an extra financial burden. Additionally, several of these artists take a great risk of being 'found out' doing something forbidden, or certainly disliked by the company direction. In spite of many difficulties, this practice has always been exercised and continues to be, with good results in general.

Throughout their studies and dancing life dancers are always taught in fairly large groups. It is not so surprising – especially when technical problems occur – that from their early student years they long to have private lessons where the teacher's attention can be focused solely on their own personal problems. Within such an intimate atmosphere pupil and master can work in a more relaxed way and, whatever the age or standard of the artist, they may be able to overcome those inhibitions and complexes which often undermine their efforts in ordinary circumstances. During private coaching a teacher also has a better opportunity to observe and understand an individual dancer's physical, mental and emotional make-up and might be able to get 'under the pupil's skin'. Faults can be detected more easily, remedies can be found and formulated to the individual's personal requirements, therefore corrections will be achieved, faster.

In all the other performing arts it has been long recognised that frequent use of the 'one-to-one' teaching method is the right way to nurture young talent. Consequently the finances and timetable schedules in these schools have been organised to accommodate this. Sadly, in our profession – particularly in the Western world – there are hardly any vocational schools where circumstances allow students to have regularly the benefits of individual coaching.

One can't really blame dancers for arranging these opportunities for themselves when they have reached independence and a position in the profession, and can afford and organise private tuition. It is perfectly understandable for them to try to fulfil a desire unsatisfied since their student days. Besides it has a reassuring effect when a dancer can work on a 'one-to-one' basis with a trusted teacher at a time of self-doubt – no matter whether it's of a technical or artistic nature – or during a period of convalescence.

If vocational schools would incorporate regular coaching and private lessons in their schedules most probably dancers would be more secure in their technique, less vulnerable to injury and, later in professional life, the physical and psychological need for private lessons would be reduced.

If, to the regular staff, additional teachers could be appointed to specialise in giving regular, sensitively conducted, private coaching, dancers would have less need to seek outside assistance. Such an arrangement worked effectively in the former Soviet ballet ensembles.

Notwithstanding, there will always be specific circumstances when artists may feel that they need a 'change' from their accustomed teachers – no matter how much private tuition they received as students or dancers, nor how successful their past and present teachers happened to be.

It is not unusual that a personality clash between an artist and a resident ballet master destroys the individual's technical and artistic progress. These dancers can't help feeling trapped in a situation which will not alter unless they seek and find some physical help and emotional support from an independent teacher of their own choice.

Other reasons should be considered. Dancers often hope – and rightly so – that being seen and corrected by a 'fresh pair of eyes' might be the solution to a technical problem. To hear a diagnosis from another expert, remedies explained from a different viewpoint, or a variant in teaching attitude and approach, could make a great deal of difference to their progress.

Also, teachers often excel at teaching in one specific field: one may succeed in conveying and correcting pirouettes better, while another perhaps can help more with elevation, fast footwork, stamina, and so on. (Needless to say, this is the same for all other artistic matters such as the interpretation of a role, the specific style of a choreographer or a period, etc.) It is natural that dancers who feel they need special attention in any of these issues should try to find a 'specialist' to help them in an atmosphere of intimacy. Singers, actors and musicians have always followed this practice to improve and perfect themselves.

Perhaps it is not so absurd – indeed, it is a very positive sign – that dancers seek so desperately for a possibility of 'one-to-one' teaching in order to better themselves in their art.

PART 3

SURVIVAL OF THE FITTEST

———————— ❖ ————————

In Spite of. . . and not Because

Mistaken ideology

One day, a principal dancer whom I had coached privately for many years burst into my studio and excitedly announced, 'I've news for you though you might not approve of it. A few hours ago I resigned from my company. I've been offered a post as ballet master to an ensemble abroad. It wasn't an easy decision but now that I have made it I feel wonderfully free, reborn, I'm leaving behind sixteen years of hard labour and maltreatment.'

'Aren't you exaggerating a bit? Surely you must have had many beautiful experiences as well?'

'Certainly I had, many of them, but this was only because I love my profession more than anything in the world. Even the management's dictatorial and brow-beating ways couldn't take away all the pleasure which dancing my roles and my audience's appreciation of them mean to me. After being so long with the company this is the first time, and the last, that I've had the opportunity and the guts to speak my mind to the director without risking losing roles, and my position. I didn't hold my tongue, I can assure you, I spoke about. . .' Out poured all the well-known complaints of dancers – the usual criticisms that I understand and sympathise with but to which I hardly need to listen, I know them all so well.

I have heard these laments so many times from countless dancers in a variety of companies. They seem to be more or less the same everywhere around the world with just a few variations according to country and company.

Suddenly my full attention was aroused. I heard him saying something unusual. 'In this company we survive – that is those of us lucky enough to do so – *in spite of* the classes we have been getting, *not because of* them as we should expect. Most of the time the teachers give routine classes, hardly ever correcting us, and the exercises are monotonous and uninspiring. Class isn't geared to our schedule and disregards our daily needs as well as our long-term requirements. Nor does this criticism apply solely to our classes but to all the other aspects of our professional life – rehearsals, casting, planning, the lot. It's a miracle that the dancers pull through in the circumstances in which they are treated by the management.'

These were very harsh words. I wondered how much truth was behind them, how much was triggered by personal bitterness, and how much was prompted by the provoked director, so I asked, 'How did your director react to your rather merciless assessment?'

'With that typical high and mighty, sarcastic and patronising manner we are so used to. "Well, my dear boy, as far as I can see, you've managed with us for sixteen years quite well, as have many others, which is the proof of the pudding. I really can't waste time in relying on those who cannot stick it out even if I feel sorry for them. I have to run a ballet company and can't do that with weaklings. I need dancers who are fit enough to cope with anything. Consider, this is a good reason why you are now a principal dancer. I bet that from now on you'll see yourself in another light and understand these things differently when you are part of a ballet management." '

I wondered if his boss's prophecy would become true? Will the same happen to him where so many ex-dancers who continued in the profession as teachers, répétiteurs, choreographers and directors slowly forget what they were up against when they were dancers? Will he also change his ideas when, as a ballet master, he will face the same issues but from a management point of view? Will he change sides completely or will he compromise sensibly? Will he become inflexible, tyrannical, or will he behave as he should: friendly but firm, motivating, challenging, demanding, but also understanding, and remembering from his dancing days what should or shouldn't be done in order to make a talented dancer's survival easier?

I heard the answers to these questions a few years later, sad ones. Indeed, he tried to stick to his guns and push his ideas through but failed against a narrow-minded, autocratic management. Finally he drowned his bitter disappointment in alcohol. This tragedy was not an unfamiliar story in our profession.

The whole argument about dancers' survival – how they do so, which kind of person is best at it, and are those who do survive the best ones who are really needed in the world of dance? – were questions which triggered in me a chain of controversial thoughts.

A long and varied experience in the dance scene has convinced me that the way we have chosen the majority of our students and dancers during the last half-century, and teach, educate, choreograph for, and treat them, could lead to a result where, generally, only the physically fittest and emotionally less vulnerable will survive and succeed.

Maybe there is nothing wrong with this. After all it is the law of nature and, whether we like it or not, this also happens in many other aspects of human activity. Why then shouldn't dance teachers also follow this as an instinctive guideline? It would make sense, especially in an occupation where so much depends on physical fitness and strength. To a certain point this might well be the correct attitude as long as we could be absolutely sure that physical suitability and undeterred willpower are not the only qualities we would look for in a dancer, even if the running of a dance company is much easier and safer with such people. The danger is that often in our profession it's not considered carefully enough that, although the fittest and the strong-minded are the most successful, this might not necessarily mean that they are the most talented individuals from an artistic point of view.

Other vitally essential questions pose themselves. Is sheer survival enough for an artist throughout a professional life? Shouldn't we care much more about the *quality* of that life? Must we agree with an opinion that the proof of the pudding is really nothing more than waiting to see which of the dancers is capable of pulling through in spite of unfavourable circumstances and treatment? Doesn't it matter how much damage they may suffer in body and mind? Could it be true that struggling for survival in this manner makes them better dancers? Is this the right path to follow in order to lengthen the relatively short period of their dancing years? Will artistic standards improve in the future if we accept this and make generations of dancers, teachers, choreographers and directors also believe that competition and survival of the fittest in the dancers' society is just as unavoidable, valid and beneficially progressive as is proven in the animal kingdom, and in business? Or are these ideas part of a mistaken ideology and attitude which may serve conveniently some short-sighted or autocratic dance managements?

To find the right answers cannot be easy but it might help if we first answer the key questions. Do we consider dancing as an art form and our dancers as artists? There is no doubt that the right answer is 'yes'. This should solve the majority of these problems.

Only the human race is capable of producing art. Animals may move their bodies by instinct in a complicated and, to the human eye, pleasing way. This is their inherited, natural way of life, a most important part of their existence and survival. Dancers use their bodies to create intricate movements of which only a small fraction is the result of natural behaviour. Much of a dancer's movement is motivated by thoughts and emotions which are the unique products of the miraculous function of the human brain. Trying to apply the laws of natural survival to a highly creative and complex life form – that of an artist, a professional dancer – appears to be misconceived. Such an idea may lead us to a mistaken ideology, and eventually to the decline of our art.

❖

Cruel to be Kind?

Encouraging emotional as well as physical development

H amlet's words to his mother: 'I must be cruel only to be kind,' have become an oft-quoted proverb for every aspect of life. If taken as a poet's advice to mankind this saying is perhaps most suitable for those in the medical and teaching professions. It is not surprising that ballet teachers, past and present, have made good use of it and the quotation has been handed down over the centuries, during which generations of dancers and teachers were brought up not even to question the validity of those words. We have learnt to respect religiously the subject material as well as the method, the ways of teaching and ideas taught to us by earlier generations.

In our profession there is also another saying – perhaps even better known and certainly colloquial – which was passed on with the best of our heritage – 'A dancer's life is tough, the sooner students get used to it, the better'. This principle was considered essential by all ballet masters who, in the past, taught only vocational students.

Ever since then all teaching methods, whether in classical or other styles, are firmly based on the idea that a dancer's body and soul must be prepared during the years of study for a pretty rough and tough lifestyle. The meaning of both these aphorisms can be interlinked easily. It seems logical that a combination of these established ideas within our teaching attitudes can produce even better results provided that these chains of thought are interpreted correctly. However, if used without thorough investigation or adaptation to given circumstances, these ideas can be misunderstood, and therefore misused with damaging consequences.

We teachers at vocational schools and within companies take great pride in conducting our classes with a certain firmness, asking for a hard, physical performance combined with quality and mental discipline. Depending on our own differing personalities, age and sex, the strictness of our demands will manifest itself in various forms. Some of us will keep a distance from our pupils while others will build up a very close and friendly relationship with them. One teacher may use humour while another may be sarcastic. Some may relate to students as an older member of a good partnership while some of us may act as a fair judge. Others can have an approach like an understanding parent, a loving sibling, or even an eccentric godparent. Whatever the different approaches dictated by our personalities the aim is the same – we wish to follow in the footsteps of our own masters and take their good advice. By requiring an uncompromisingly high standard in our classes we want to make sure that we will adequately prepare and toughen our students and young dancers for a career which is difficult and demanding.

We occasionally come across certain dance teachers who like to boast with pride about keeping rigorous discipline and hardship in class. From the classroom we hear, as if from a battlefield, their screaming, yelling and raving. They often punish and threaten students with demands for harder physical tasks. They may even extend class time and, in doing so, deprive students of their break – a period for recovery, rest and nourishment. In the staff room they say with satisfaction, 'I gave them hell! They won't be able to move tomorrow. That'll toughen up this lazy lot.' If someone, disapproving of this militant behaviour, should ask, 'But what will you do tomorrow in class with those stiff and aching bodies?' and then dares to add the word 'souls', the answer might be, 'Work them just as hard and if they sulk, then even harder! This'll teach them that dancer's beds are not made of roses.' Indeed this would, certainly for those few lucky ones whose bodies (though not souls) survive this kind of overdrive without injury or ugly and heavy-looking muscles. But, what will happen to those students who drop out because of this misguided toughening treatment? They may well be very talented youngsters who, at this stage of their studies, haven't yet built up much durability. Can our art form afford to let this happen?

There are other not-so-bellicose teachers who argue that it is good to push pupils who, being young, strong, eager, and familiar with the proverbs in question, expect to be toughened and relish being driven beyond their limits. This is often true, especially with male students. It is also true that if the overwork is a consequence of a mutual enthusiasm and not used as a disciplinary punishment, the students' vulnerability to injury will be far less as there will be no disturbing mental strain. Nevertheless the probability of dancers' bodies being hurt is at its highest level when they are challenged beyond their limits. Even if the students voluntarily force themselves over their maximum level the risk of harming the body is still high and so is the possibility of misshaping the muscles. Ambitious young students won't necessarily know how much is too much, or how some old, wise saying should be correctly put into practice. It is the teacher who should know better and explain to pupils that even enjoying overwork doesn't necessarily mean that it will be beneficial to them in the long run. There are several other aspects of our profession where the above sayings are often quoted out of context.

In most vocational schools around the world students are expected to wear uniforms, especially in ballet classes. They are not allowed to wear any type of leg-warmer or additional top over official tights and leotard. The reasons behind these rules are important and obvious. Firstly, it is essential that both teacher and students should be able to see muscle-work, body lines, and any possible increase or decrease of weight clearly and immediately, without obstruction from heavy, wrinkling materials.. Secondly, it is thought that in order to keep their muscles warm students will work harder and more constantly during class if they are wearing only a thin uniform. These points are valid in countries with a warm climate, and also where the schools can provide well-heated and draught-proof classrooms, dressing-rooms and corridors during the cold season. Alas, this is hardly ever the case, so these sensible ideas which should serve students' progress become the cause of increased risk of injury and may hinder the healing of existing aches and pains.

Nowadays, in most vocational schools, besides classical ballet and character dance studies, other disciplines such as jazz, contemporary and tap-dancing are included in the curriculum. Ideally, these varied styles of dancing require differently maintained floors. Unfortunately, privately run establishments can seldom provide separate practice rooms with correctly treated floors according to the needs of each discipline. Thus students and teachers constantly struggle with floors which are either slippery or too tacky. Both extremes hinder progress and could easily become dangerous health hazards.

Partly to solve these problems and partly because of the ever-growing number of dance students many schools are building additional studios or moving into new or larger premises. The latter are usually converted buildings originally constructed for completely different purposes. In spite of the great cost, studio floors are often laid wrongly because of mistaken advice given by experts. The outcome of this can sadly become the dancers' greatest enemy – the hard floor.

Recognising these hazards, medical experts often back up the students with requests to alter regulations which appear senseless and harmful, or to update heating systems and to take more care about floor maintenance. Caring, open-minded teachers are also usually in total agreement about these basic requirements but, more often than not, their opinions are overruled and they are quickly put into place by other staff. 'Nonsense! We mustn't molly-coddle these spoilt youngsters. They'll have to deal with much worse in the future with all those draughty, slippery and hard stages, ice-cold dressing-rooms and corridors. It's in their own interests to become tough and learn to cope with it.' If someone dared to argue that it still seems a bit harsh, even cruel, though there may be a lot of truth in what is said, the answer may be once again, 'Well, sometimes you must be cruel to be kind.' To use the quotation in this context might seem all too convenient.

In the many years of a student's life, especially those of a boarder, it happens from time to time that students disobey rules or misbehave. They get out of hand and certain disciplinary measures must be taken. Sometimes we get carried away by this and we punish them unjustly or too severely. We may easily misjudge a situation and make the innocent majority suffer for the misbehaviour of the few. Later, when we realise our mistake, many of us will feel somewhat guilty and will seek a way to correct the injustice. In doing so we often find that some members of staff are of the opinion that the reaction is not only unnecessary but actually unwise. 'Undeserved punishment won't do them any harm. Let them swallow the bitter pill. When they become professionals they'll often be treated unfairly. They'll be in and out of favour, and their self-confidence and pride will be cruelly crushed. Such is a dancers' life and we'd better get them used to it right away.'

Indeed, for a dancer to survive in the rough, stormy and treacherous seas of vanity, whims and intrigues, can be difficult and disheartening. Many haven't got enough inner strength to fight and overcome these falsehoods, power struggles and scandals successfully. One of the most important tasks of a teacher is not only to prepare dancers' bodies for survival even in the most trying circumstances but their minds and souls as well. The question arises, what is the best way to do all this? Should we subject our students – bodies and souls – to rough and unfair treatment; in other words, should we create a miniature hell in order to prepare them for a real one? Do we really have to be cruel in order to be kind and, if so, should it be within this context? Isn't this a misconceived exaggeration of an aphorism conveniently to evade problems?

Survival in our profession generally isn't harder than in any other vocation. Life for everyone is difficult and often unjust, full of suffering and sometimes with horrors. Parents and teachers in every walk of life should tell the younger generation not only about the good and beautiful things around them but also about the difficulties and ugly side of life: cruelty, falsehood, wretchedness and so on. But should we make them experience all these things during their student years just in order that they can stand up to things whenever, and if ever, they come across them in adulthood? In ordinary life we all wish to be good parents but would we beat, abuse, cheat, torture, overwork and injure our own children for these reasons?

Perhaps we can understand the necessity and validity of this kind of teaching attitude in connection with the training of soldiers. Their feelings, indeed, must be toughened against injury just as much as their bodies to endure all the horrors of war.

Considering that artists need to develop great sensitivity and intensity of feelings it seems that to anaesthetise a dancer's emotional life may result in more and more robot-like performers instead of susceptible, refined artists.

We teachers are doing exactly what the old saying suggests when we correct or assess our students, or when we fail them in examinations, also when we criticise dancers for a meaningless interpretation or a bad performance, and when we have to tell some of them about their untheatrical demeanour – possibly due to excess weight, skinniness, a too-big nose, overdeveloped muscles, etc. We are delivering the cruel truth to our pupils in order to help them in their career. To prepare our students physically for our so-called 'tough' vocation we need to make sure that a disciplined and consistent practice which stretches their abilities to their limits (and not beyond them!) will help them to achieve maximum durability and stamina while injuries to their bodies are kept to an absolute minimum.

The best mental preparation for young dancers' professional lives is to build up devotion, respect and pride towards the art of dance, to help them to find their own identity and strengthen their self-confidence. This may be a far better defence against all kinds of insult and maltreatment which they may suffer as young adults rather than over-challenging and provoking them whilst they are only students. Finally, we must constantly remind ourselves that in today's vocational schools a great many of the students may never become dancers. Why should these youngsters be put through so much unnecessary physical and mental injury? Why shouldn't they have the joy that a dance experience can give them?

In our teaching attitudes we must not indiscriminately follow popular sayings just because they are part of the tradition, without carefully re-examining and revalidating them. The meaning of our colloquial sayings can provide useful guidelines but only if we adapt them specifically and use them in the correct connection and right circumstances.

---❖---

That Extra Spark . . . called Talent

Talent can be overlooked

To achieve a high standard and good progress in dance depends on three main factors. One of these is how well professional skills and artistic qualities are conveyed to students – in short, on the teachers' talents to educate. Another factor is how early achievements are preserved and revitalised in teaching and in the unpolluted interpretation of the great classics – in short, on the teachers', répétiteurs' and dancers' talents, knowledge and style. Much rests also on how fresh ideas and daring experiments in new styles are included in teaching, in interpretation and in composition by each generation – in short, on the teachers', dancers' and choreographers' talents, intelligence, personality and maturity.

To start with, the finding and choice of all these talents are up to teachers, school directors and examiners, and the principal criteria they use when choosing from amongst the prospective candidates as they are about to enter vocational schools, and later when at school these students are examined, assessed and sorted out. After graduation the right choice will depend on the artistic taste and priority of a ballet master, company director or choreographer when auditioning the dancers for professional engagements. The final filtering process comes with casting for particular roles.

To help those responsible in this delicate and important task there are some internationally well-known fundamental guidelines. Several of these established ideas are based on traditional practice and experience, and on the recommendations from experts in modern medical science. But a great part depends on the adjudicators' own personal observations of human nature, on their artistic principles, aesthetic preferences and intuition. The ideal solution for finding the right type of dancer – *not only the fittest to survive but also the best* – is to bring all these different viewpoints together, though this usually proves to be the hardest and most responsible task amongst our duties. Some of the difficulties arise because members of the auditioning committee have conflicting opinions about the qualities of the candidates. Artistic viewpoints may clash with medical ones, traditional ideas with modern considerations, or one personal view with another. In addition to these difficulties there is another which complicates things even more. Assessments should be made not only about the physical suitability of these unformed youngsters – on which one can make numerous mistakes – but, at the same time, we ought to be able to assess their psychological make-up and talent.

It is not easy to recognise artistic talent. We know very little of how the 'extra spark' develops and at what age it might manifest itself, as this is still unknown to science. Some youngsters, if skilfully auditioned, might well show signs of being musical, expressive, extrovert, determined or meticulous; qualities which are all necessary ingredients for an artistic personality. But even if some candidates possess most or all of these and are able to bring them to the surface when required, it still may not necessarily mean that they have that 'extra spark' which we call talent. Also, some children when under examination and stress may become timid, nervous and withdrawn, incapable of showing just those gifts for which the auditioning committee is looking.

At later stages the pitfalls in the so-called 'weeding-out' process at examinations are due to the external examiners not knowing the students at all. However, those systems which are based on assessments by external examiners are generally less destructive to a pupil's future for two reasons. Firstly, because in the case of a failure the candidate always has a chance to try again with a different examiner. Secondly, even in the event of a failure at the last attempt, pupils are not necessarily advised to give up dancing as a career. They may continue at their vocational school and, with time, might well become dancers.

In contrast, for those teachers who as staff members fulfil the role of examiner within vocational schools, making these important assessments at regular intervals might be easier when they have known or taught the students for many years. On the other hand their opinion will carry a much greater responsibility; a student's ejection from a vocational school could be final, and tragically irreversible.

There are further complications which neither external examiners nor internal teachers may be able to escape. Important decisions are made at a period when dance students are going through disturbing years of puberty, so their emotional reactions could be unpredictable and often misleading. It is not surprising that at auditions, exams, and other similar assessments and selections, some talents may be misjudged, either because some superficial qualities are mistaken for the real thing or because potential abilities may be deeply hidden under a psychologically protected surface and overlooked at a time of stress.

Of course teachers and examiners in other art forms have to face similar problems on these occasions but, as we all know, what makes our situation different and twice as difficult is the fact that dancing is a physical art and dancers' instruments are their own bodies. When a young candidate's potential is being judged a considerable amount of attention must be given to their physical appearance. When we audition, examine or assess youngsters we not only have to find and judge characteristics and qualities for future artists but simultaneously we have to judge their future instruments as well. We need to make sure that each dancer, when the time comes, will have an instrument which is beautiful and strong enough to promote the success of its artist/owner's survival. It is just the same as a musical audition where the committee in charge would need to examine not only the young musician's talent and playing skills but at the same time the quality and endurance of the piano, 'cello, trumpet, oboe or whichever instrument on which the student plays.

This essential need to focus on the physique of a potential dancer is the reason why our responsibility is doubled, and it can also be the source from which the majority of mistakes may stem. One can become easily preoccupied with the importance of physical factors, putting the artistic requirements in second place or even neglecting them altogether.

Taking all these issues into consideration and the fact that most of these decisions have to be made at a time when the candidate is essentially immature, some misjudgement is unavoidable, and very regrettable. Indeed, dance history has proved time and time again that a dancer's mind, talent and willpower are capable of producing unexpected achievements which can influence and over-come physical restrictions. Some imperfections of bodily beauty can sink into insignificance when overtaken by outstanding artistic values. The list of examples is endless, full of extraordinary stories of unpredictable progress and regress, successful survival or total failure which far outnumber those occurring in other art forms.

We should admit that the errors made in selection and assessment cause more serious problems in the profession than meet the eye, on one side losing real talents, on the other wasting precious time and devoted work on the wrong type of student. In addition to the unnecessary stress and disappointment for all the teachers involved, and for the many unfortunate youngsters and their parents, the results of erroneous selection must bring stagnation in artistic standards.

It's important that we try to find a way to reduce the number of errors made during these vital selection activities; in order to do this successfully we should find the causes, the wrong ideas and attitudes which often lead us astray. Is it possible that some of these misleading thoughts are just the ones which are closely connected with the most important ideas about dancers' survival? After all, the whole point of auditions and exams is that through them we should be able to find the type of personality and physique that is the most suitable for the profession.

We should look out for those whose physical, intellectual and artistic qualities will ensure that they survive the student years as well as the professional life, youngsters on whom long periods of teaching will not be wasted and on whose accomplishments a dance company's work can safely rely. We need to make sure that we are not sidetracked by assuming that all is well because in the end the physically and mentally fittest will survive anyway.

Perhaps we should try and seek different, better, newer methods, complementing and improving the old ones, and spend more time and thought when choosing, examining and selecting candidates by searching for those who have got that 'extra spark' and who, with wise teaching and good treatment, will become fit enough, not only to survive but to thrive for the benefit of our profession.

Dancing begins in the brain

Since my student days I have heard many stories about great dancers from the beginning of this century, often from people who saw them performing, read descriptions of their dancing or viewed photographs and old movies. I have often wondered how many of them would be given the chance nowadays even to start studying in a vocational school attached to a company, let alone to become professional dancers and to rise to stardom. As a student, dancer and teacher I had to learn about the significance of the correct proportions of a dancer's body from both an aesthetic and an anatomical point of view. Later, I also came to realise that many legendary dancers, and also quite a number of famous stars today, would fail to meet these norms.

Once, in a dance history class, we were learning about the Diaghilev Ballets Russes company and its great achievements and we looked at pictures of the dancers. This was the first time I had ever seen a photograph of Vaslav Nijinsky and I couldn't believe my eyes. I'd never seen this dance phenomenon in action and, being young and preoccupied with the importance of the lean, long lines of a dancer's body, I expected to see a tall, Apollo-like, perfect and beautiful physique, something quite common even amongst the unknown male dancers of any *corps de ballet*. Instead, I was looking at a portrait of a rather short figure with quite unfavourable proportions. A big head was perched on a relatively long torso to which short, heavy-looking arms and legs were attached, covered with well-developed muscles. Was this what the Blue God, the Spirit of the Rose, the Golden Slave, the one-and-only idol of so many people, looked like? Today, a dancer of his height and proportions, even with a most outstanding technique, would be allowed to dance only character or *demi-caractère* roles, certainly not the kind of repertoire for which Nijinsky became famous and which elevated him to the status of a semi-god.

One of my fellow students was of the opinion that the key to Nijinsky's incredible technical achievements might well have been his extraordinary proportions and those over-developed leg muscles. They included his famous, unusually long Achilles tendons which enabled him to achieve his flight-like elevation. Our teacher explained that though this great dancer had an astonishing ballon, and a very strong, all-round technique, what really made him unique was not just his virtuosity but his extraordinary quality, a many-faceted and sensitive artistry and, above all, his magical stage presence.

'He must have been very fortunate,' expressed another colleague, 'that Diaghilev had the kind of extraordinary eye that could spot the genius within that strange-looking body.'

Nijinsky must have had everything indeed: immense technique, flair, as well as the good fortune to be discovered in the right place and at the right time. However, I hardly guessed what I strongly suspect now, that his real luck actually started when, as a child, he escaped rejection by the auditioning committee of the Imperial

Ballet School in St Petersburg. Though the young Nijinsky looked and behaved awkwardly, Nicolai Legat noticed his unusual muscle structure, and consequently his jumping potential, and persuaded the rest of the adjudicators to give a chance to the son of the fabulous dancer, Foma Nijinsky.

His luck continued at school when he evaded being 'weeded out', in spite of not fitting in with his classmates, having strange proportions and being rather slow in intellectual development. His wonderful teachers, the Legat brothers and Mikhail Obukov, helped, encouraged and gave him the chance to develop into the technical phenomenon and unique artist whom Diaghilev would discover and promote to a stardom so far unparalleled in the ballet world.

His luck was everybody's good fortune. For him it meant becoming what he wanted to be and much more. For the Ballets Russes, to have such a star among them helped the fame of the ensemble to grow rapidly. For his male colleagues, he was a genuine and incomparable rival who challenged and raised their standards. For the choreographers, designers and composers, he was an inspiration through his talent and capability. For his audience, his magical performances suddenly revolutionised an art form to an extent unequalled ever before. For posterity, dancers and balletomanes today can enjoy and learn from the results of his influence on a great number of twentieth-century dancers, choreographers, designers, painters and musicians.

What an incredible loss it would have been for the art of ballet if this exceptional talent had been turned away from a dancing career on account of his unpleasing proportions, not fitting in, and being a bit odd and slow in his intellect. Still, I wonder whether he would be accepted today in any company-connected vocational school?

Nijinsky's case, as far as his unusual body proportion was concerned, was just a question of aesthetic taste and had nothing to do with weakness or possible vulnerability to injury. Therefore it was not a matter of physical survival. But there were numerous, more complicated and medically involved examples in dance history where a dancer's ability and achievements have proved to be exactly the opposite to what common sense, the knowledge of anatomy, dance technique and dance medicine could have ever predicted.

Since I started teaching professional dancers, and have seen so many gifted young artists struggle with all kinds of minor bodily restrictions or defects, I often asked myself what would my

reaction have been if I had been in charge at the Imperial Ballet
School when, for example, Olga Preobrajenska auditioned for
admittance as a pupil? Would I have thought it wise even to let her
start, let alone to allow her to continue her studies? Would I have
seen any possibility for a girl to succeed as a dancer when she was
actually suffering from several physical defects and weaknesses
that must have been quite obvious at the time of her audition?
Defects which today would be more than enough to deter a young
candidate from taking up dancing as a vocation.

'Hunchbacked devil' was the horribly cruel nickname given to
Preobrajenska by her famous teacher Christian Johannson when
she was already an adolescent. The scoliosis from which she
suffered forced her to wear a steel corset, day and night, for a
whole year and certainly wasn't the kind of 'hardly noticeable'
defect which often occurs amongst dance students and which can
be easily compensated for by exercises. The deformation of her
spine must have been quite an eyesore.

As a young pupil she also suffered from general ill health and
often had to miss her ballet classes for long periods. Her feet were
weak and one of her knees was much more sway backed than the
other. As a result her pointe work was quite inadequate for years.
In stature she was much shorter than her classmates and rather
plumpish. Who in their right mind and with a responsible attitude
would give a chance to such a candidate?

Indeed, during her school years, she wasn't welcomed by
teachers and was twice dismissed, then readmitted. The only
reason for this seemingly completely unsuited child to be taken in
the school and then kept on as an adolescent, was that she
happened to be the protégée of a very influential actress. How
distressing it must have been for the young girl to be constantly
discouraged. She was considered ugly, weak and malformed by
both teachers and schoolmates yet she proved everybody wrong.
She showed everyone that if Fate hadn't given her an influential
protector and a chance to become a dancer, the dance world would
have lost one of its greatest artists and teachers.

With immense willpower, the weak, hunchbacked devil transformed herself into a very strong technician and one of the finest,
most expressive and lyrical performers in the history of dance. Her
unique qualities inspired, amongst others, the genius of Mikhail
Fokine. In his masterpiece, Chopiniana (Les Sylphides), the
'Prelude', a most sensitive solo, was created for Preobrajenska's
refined, poetical lyricism. Today it is considered to be a turning

point and the cornerstone of modern choreography.

To achieve the strength and stamina required by a ballerina, she taught herself how to compensate for and overcome her bodily defects and weaknesses. Besides diligence, perseverance and very hard work, she made much use of her own natural intelligence, far more than other more healthy dancers would do, and she had hardly any help from her teachers until, in her later years, she met Enrico Cecchetti.

'Dancing begins in the brain' she used to say, and she certainly proved the truth of this both as a dancer and teacher. To overcome her shortcomings she instinctively taught herself movement analysis and discovered special remedial and strengthening exercises. Invaluable knowledge gained through her experiences as performer and pedagogue were passed on to help and influence a vast number of dancers, teachers and choreographers.

Preobrajenska achieved more than just fame as a ballerina with an exceptional quality and technique and as an extraordinary teacher, because she became an outstanding example to the entire profession. She is proof of what real talent is all about – something we still don't adequately know how to recognise. Additionally her case proves that sometimes what professionals may find displeasing or repulsive in a dancer's body is of no concern to an audience, which after all should be the real judge. Preobrajenska was loved and cherished by her audience, for being just what she was, an artist. The public didn't even notice or mind about scoliosis, swayback knees, or any other deficiencies.

Her career wasn't just a sheer struggle against all odds, it was a successful survival of a most worthy talent to everyone's benefit. Her example has made many teachers understand how physical restrictions and deficiencies can sometimes be overcome by psychological means, intellect, talent and willpower.

When we are searching for those rare qualities which are part of a real talent and help dancers to survive and to be successful, nothing could be more uplifting than to know the astonishing history of Olga Preobrajenska as well as stories of numerous other, lesser-known, dancers with similar but less complex problems. It helps teachers in their work to assist, reassure and animate constantly worried students and dancers that the possibility of overcoming some of the physical problems from which they suffer might be solved by their own determination and intelligence.

Glass or Diamond

Craftsman or artist?

Encouraging, comforting, reassuring, challenging and stimulating vocational students and professional dancers are just as important a part of a teacher's task as actual tuition, and in some special cases are needed even more. The necessity for us to do all this becomes even more apparent, especially in professional open classes and private lessons, when we come across many of those dancers whose talent might be of 'silver', 'gold' or even 'diamond' standard, but for some odd reason it was brushed aside as 'tin', 'brass' or 'glass'.

At one of my open classes a very beautiful dancer introduced herself. She wished to take private lessons with me in addition to open classes whenever her recent *corps de ballet* engagement with a leading ballet company would allow her the time.

She must have ambition and willpower, and be diligent as well, I thought, if she wishes to extend her heavy schedule with so much extra work. From the very first *plié* exercise it became pretty obvious that she had exceptional quality and musicality, just enough turn-out in her perfectly proportioned physique but, surprisingly, superficial schooling. Her placement was faulty and therefore her technique was unreliable, and her muscles appeared to have developed unevenly. She had a natural, fast and extremely light elevation but was not well co-ordinated with her *ports de bras*. Her beautiful feet were fairly strong on *pointes* but in adage she was too weak to control and hold extensions which were not very high anyway, and as far as her *pirouettes* were concerned – well, they didn't exist.

She simply wasn't strong enough to be up to the standard of an average *corps de ballet* dancer. The fact that she was taken into a company mainly on the merit of her artistic qualities and physical beauty pleasantly surprised me but I was disturbed because I couldn't understand why her technique was so inadequate.

I surmised that her weakness might be due to some long-lasting illness or injury, or that she might have started her ballet studies at a later age than usual, but these guesses turned out to be wrong. What could have been the matter with her? Why, after some seven years of study in private vocational schools, did she still look like an 'uncut diamond'? Was she lazy, or just unintelligent, too dim to understand and carry out corrections?

After a few private lessons and some short discussions I found that none of these suppositions would fit her character and mental capacity. She was in fact very diligent, bright, even witty, inquisitive and interested in other art forms as well as life in general. She was very well read and, above all, entirely devoted to her profession. She responded to corrections very positively, almost too much so as she had a strong inclination to ridicule herself.

'Nothing's right with my body – placement, turn-out, extensions, strength or technique,' she said after her first private lesson. 'I really don't understand at all how I managed to get into this company. All I know is that I desperately want to become a dancer and now I have a chance. If you think that I am not an utterly hopeless case, please, would you help me to make sure that I will be good enough not to get the boot?'

This was the beginning of a long-lasting, extremely interesting, challenging, very rewarding and most successful teacher-artist relationship. She didn't get the sack, far from it. After many years of intensive work she has become one of the most promising, versatile ballerinas of her company, who, even as a young soloist, inspired choreographers to create new ballets for her and now her interpretations of some well-known classical, romantic, lyrical and poetical roles are widely admired by public and critics alike.

During the many years that we have worked together I have found out more details about her character as well as the history of her student years, and gradually the pieces of this jigsaw puzzle fit together. Her progress as a dancer and as an artist was uneven, and proceeded in a different order from that of a typical dancer. She achieved mental and emotional maturity and artistic sensitivity at a much younger age than usual, while her progress in physical strength and technical perfection took place at a much slower speed. Probably her unusual, though not unique, way of developing was the reason why, as a child, she was 'weeded out' after the first few terms of study at a leading vocational school. The reasons given for her dismissal were that her physique was hopelessly weak and that her personality was difficult as she was too 'cerebral'. She was different from the preconceived ideal child of most ballet schools.

Why, at that tender age, did she appear unsuited to the profession of a dancer? First: at the age of ten this child's body, though slim and well proportioned, simply wasn't fit enough. She was considered to be *too weak* to survive as a performer. (One can't help wondering if seven or eight years of good schooling might just solve such a problem?) Second: she was too brainy, too inquisitive. She's the type of dancer who needs to have certain movements analysed and broken down into smaller sections in order for her to execute them properly. She feels uneasy and physically unsafe when just copying and repeating steps mechanically. She has to understand exactly what she is expected to do before her physique will obey, therefore she keeps asking questions. It is rather unusual for a youngster to approach dancing in this manner but it is essentially positive and beneficial to the gradual unfolding of an artist's personality.

If this young girl and her parents had accepted the recommendation of a respected panel of teachers and taken their advice, this unusual but greatly admired dancer would have been lost to the world of dance. Fortunately neither parents nor child gave up hope and decided to have a further try.

Like other families in similar circumstances they searched for other schools and private teachers who would help the girl's undeterred devotion and willpower. Nevertheless, in spite of all the support from her parents and her teachers at private schools, the fact remained that she was deprived of the best possible tuition and the ideal curriculum which she needed, and deserved, in order to follow the usual route leading from a vocational school directly to a connected company. Besides the problem of how to overcome her physical weakness in less than ideal circumstances, she had an even more serious one – she had to heal and forget the serious psychological trauma suffered from an early rejection. The complete loss of self-confidence and her physical weakness had to be remedied simultaneously. As a result she lost a great deal of precious time in her career.

Even today, though strong, appreciated and successful, she still has the scars of her emotional injuries. From time to time she battles with an old, debilitating enemy – an inferiority complex – yet her survival proves that it might not necessarily be the fittest who remain for the true benefit of our art.

Her story shows that the best dancers – those who possess a

real talent for dancing and a determination for successful endurance – are often disguised within different shapes and forms and their talents don't manifest themselves in an obvious and predictable manner or in the usual space of time.

Finding diamonds means hard work: searching for them, having expert eyes to spot them even if they appear in the most unlikely forms and circumstances, and making sure that we don't dismiss them as valueless shards of glass.

On the other hand it is just as important that we don't mistake some good-looking, shiny glass for a true gem. This can happen easily, especially at preliminary auditions when choosing a child with a well-proportioned body and good mobility who proves later to have little artistic potential behind the promising exterior. If the error is discovered soon and the right remedy taken the harm done is fairly insignificant. However, a chain of real trouble starts when the mistake is overlooked for too long a time.

Just as good craftsmen can cut and polish glass to a convincing imitation, intelligent and well-meaning teachers can utilise their professional skills to make a suitable physique move with pleasing precision. If a student is taught and polished with consistent care for many years by knowledgeable pedagogues the result can easily be a perfect 'fake'. One might ask 'So what, if the fake looks and dances as well as the genuine talent, who cares?' Though not really talented but with some feeling for style, nor truly musical but able to keep in time with the music, nor very expressive but intelligent enough to learn the basic technique of mime and theatrical gestures, and possessing a pleasing looking body and face in addition to perseverance, this imitation of a genuinely gifted dancer will pass quite well for a real one. However, it does matter!

Dancers, when joining a company, usually start in the corps de ballet. As long as they are pleasing to the eye, well-trained, stylish and disciplined, they will do a good job. That is exactly what it will be – a *job* done by good craftsmen – but do we really want to saturate our dance companies with good-looking artisans doing satisfactory jobs in the *corps*, or should we have talented artists dancing even in the lower ranks of an ensemble? Isn't this an important factor by which we can measure the true standards of a dance company?

Furthermore, some of the best-working and fittest 'artisan' dancers who first fill the *corps* will be tried out in some solo work. Due to their physical suitability most of them will function adequately in their technically more-demanding solo roles.

Eventually, quite a few of them may become *coryphées*, soloists, and even leading dancers. Before we realise it, dance companies could be packed with these reliable, adequate, hard-working dancers. Probably they will be capable of doing *good jobs*, yielding technically faultless performances. They will shine as well-prepared glass can, but they will never have the glittering dazzle and real value of diamonds.

By mastering the techniques, one can conduct an orchestra, play a musical instrument, sing, dance or declaim a role with faultless precision, but a real talent will not only perform correctly but will always add a personal quality. This unique personal magnetism is the creative and artistic part of the interpretative arts; it adds magic to craft, transforms craftsmanship into artistic interpretation. Without it dance performances will be reduced to cold, spiritless and meaningless illustrations of steps and gestures which leave the audience untouched. Choreographers will be frustrated and uninspired in attempting new creations.

Generally it takes between seven and nine years of devoted work to produce a competent graduate, and another four to five years of polishing within a company to perfect a good professional dancer. One cannot but wish that all this effort could be showered on real talents whose inspired dancing revitalises our art instead of being wasted on people who, through no fault of their own, turn it into a mere skill and cause our profession to decline. The perceptive audience can become gradually disillusioned and we may lose them; a different public will admire and demand the thrill of sheer physical virtuosity and dazzling acrobatic tricks without understanding or appreciating the traditions, style, refinement and deeper meaning of true dancing. It will be an audience hardly touched by artistic experiences.

Inevitably, a few of these 'artisan' dancers will slip through the net of the auditioning and examining teachers. This happens in the other performing arts too, but what gives cause for serious concern is the increasing number of these cases. There must be other ways to make the net finer. We should react with more sensitivity to those misleading signs shown by some of the candidates while discovering hidden but genuine qualities in others.

There are many different, new ideas which examiners and auditioning committee members might consider worth trying out. One possibility is in having a preliminary period of observation prior to young candidates' auditions and examinations, so that panel members can become more familiar with the children – and vice versa. Another might be to invite a child psychologist to take part in the observation during this period as well as at the time of actual auditions. Having the benefit of such expert advice, in addition to the traditional tests, we should have a better chance of identifying artistic talent. It would be useful for all teachers, particularly those with a responsibility for auditioning, selecting, examining and assessing, to be more familiar with certain aspects of psychology when dealing with artistic children and adolescents.

Though this kind of approach could be very helpful in finding genuine talent, the situation may not change unless those in charge of selective activities re-examine their convictions about the absolute priority of physical fitness and attach equal importance to the intellectual and emotional make-up of an artist in their judgements. Only when these two faculties interact can a true dancer be created.

PART 4

THE ART OF TEACHING

---❖---

Correction and Praise

The general atmosphere of our classes has a great influence on the progress of our students. Creating an artistic atmosphere will not only enhance self-discipline and devotion from students but it will also bring about much higher standards. Nevertheless, it is easy to make mistakes unknowingly and ruin all the good effort by ignoring some very important factors. I have watched and, as a former dancer, have participated in some beautifully structured classes which were conducted by the teacher with great artistry. The exercises were explained with great clarity and in a pleasant manner, and the classes were supported by a high-quality musical accompaniment. What else could one ask for? Yet the atmosphere was often far from inspiring. Even if the pupils showed no sign of boredom or lack of concentration, it was obvious that something was wrong.

There are several reasons why the general mood of a class, even in ideal circumstances, can become negative. Whatever the cause, the roots of the problem are often the same. They arise from the relationship between the teacher and the students. We all know that besides teaching the subject material a dance teacher's most important task is to give corrections, constantly. I remember how in my early teaching days – and the same has happened to so many other young and eager teachers – I showered my poor students with an endless number of corrections and felt immensely satisfied.

We have to consider that in each class we must first communicate the exercises, enchaînements and any new material. These have to be taught and the pupils must have time to memorise and then practise them. This is quite a time-consuming process. The young teacher feels there is hardly any time left for giving all the necessary corrections for the many faults seen in a well-populated class.

In addition to the pressing time factor we are also very much aware that to stop dancers too often, even to analyse their movements, is unhealthy. It can result in misshapen muscles and injuries. So we are left giving students a list of their faults but with no time for even a few words of approval.

I must have taught like this for some time before I noticed that the majority of my pupils, a group of girls aged between thirteen and fifteen, had become nervous and inhibited. They started to dance awkwardly with tense bodies and stiff limbs. Gradually the more ambitious students became increasingly depressed, while the less eager ones lost interest and became somewhat apathetic. Naturally, as the class atmosphere took a turn for the worse the dance standards dropped dramatically and the number of minor injuries noticeably grew.

I wanted to change this situation for the better so, in desperation, I tried to teach even more conscientiously, so I thought, and kept on with even more corrections – obviously, as there was now even more to criticise. That brought on even more depression, apathy, tears and dramas.

Understandably, but quite wrongly, I started to become impatient with my students, often losing my temper as well as my confidence in their ability, and my own. This vicious circle seemed to be complete until, one day, I found enough courage to talk these problems over with my students.

From their timid, and not always too explicit, but definitely honest remarks and hints their simple message gradually came home to me. Hearing all the time from their teacher only about their shortcomings and hardly ever about their merits, they first found their self-confidence crushed to pieces, and later they lost confidence in my competence, too. Unknowingly, I had set the scene for a feeling of absolute hopelessness. How could one possibly have positive artistic and energetic activity from teenagers in classes where the pupils feel desperately inadequate?

Of course, unjustified appraisal or constant approval without balancing them with corrections can be just as harmful and, funnily enough, has the same result in the long run. The number of times I've heard dancers and students saying, 'I thought I must have been doing very well because I got a lot of appreciation from my teacher. This was very encouraging until I noticed that I and my classmates were praised when it wasn't very much deserved, so I can't trust my teacher's judgement any more.' Then they begin to believe that their dancing must be awful and don't even know what corrections they need or where to turn for guidance.

So, we have to face the same result again, the loss of hope for a student's own progress and lack of confidence in the teacher. There are some of us who seemingly solve these problems which have arisen through either over-correcting or over-praising. I'm often approached by dancers to give them help in private lessons because, as they tell me, they do have very good classes but there is no time for corrections. When I try to cheer them up by saying, 'At least you can't complain that your self-confidence is getting crushed,' they answer that being told off or criticised may not be pleasant but at least they know that they are being noticed, that one is important enough to be corrected.

Indeed, not being noticed for a while in classes eventually makes a dancer feel insignificant, and later invisible. Can anyone imagine anything worse happening to an interpretative artist of a visual art form than to feel invisible? How long will it be before this takes its toll on stage or, for younger students, at assessment classes and examinations? How many vulnerable talents will withdraw into their shells because they are unable to cope with this insensitive treatment? It is alarming how the mistakes of our teaching attitudes can result in the more sensitive and talented amongst our pupils being lost to the profession. For teachers at all levels it is difficult but essential to find the right balance: when and how much to correct and to praise. We should search for our own mistakes, admit them openly and change our way of teaching.

Though it was a bitter experience, I consider that I was very lucky to have learnt from my poor, depressed pupils, in my early teaching days, at least how not to do it. I learnt also that children and adults can obviously take much more correction and criticism than youngsters in puberty. This is very important and must not be belittled – the greater bulk of teaching the technical skills of dance happens just at that period of a dancer's life. One can't just brush aside the fact that everything that happens to students at this age leaves a very deep impression on their mental progress. This will affect their artistry tremendously in their future career.

Finally, I also learnt that no matter what age group or gender one is teaching, talking problems over with one's students is crucial and might teach one a lot. A close relationship with them, knowing more about them and their ways of seeing problems will build up friendship, mutual understanding and trust. Whenever possible a teacher's motto should be:

Today you have done better than yesterday but tomorrow you will do even better.

❖

Harmful Corrections

Just nerves

Most of us have agonising memories from our dancing years when, in class or especially in rehearsal, we were given some technical task that, no matter how hard we tried, we failed to perfect. Often the problem was temporary, perhaps occurring on an 'off' day and on the next day it would be all right, but sometimes it could become an annoyance which hounded one's life. We would work on it every single day to master it, often in vain. If one day we finally achieved it, the next day we might have lost it again. The more feverishly we practised, the worse it became. Unless one was fortunate to receive good advice immediately the problem arose, a simple technical challenge could easily grow out of all proportion and become a real ordeal.

One felt so foolish, utterly unsuited, ashamed and angry. If one had any self-esteem, this was surely the time to lose it entirely. One feared the moment when the dreaded combination of steps, *pirouettes* or a lift had to be faced and fought again during the daily routine, and even worse was the agonising experience of being obliged to perform it on stage. It's hardly imaginable that this upsetting situation could become even worse but often it did and for the most unexpected reason – being given too much advice!

This may seem illogical and contradictory. After all what better solution could there be than being helped by an unbiased and experienced professional such as a teacher, répétiteur, choreographer or just a colleague? In a company everyone is familiar with this situation as most dancers have been in a similar state, and it is natural that professionals want to come to the rescue when they notice someone needs help.

To begin with, usually only the teacher or choreographer who set the technical task in the first place notices that the dancer has a problem and the advice and correction are always gratefully received. However, if there is no satisfactory result, after a little while other staff members and colleagues will notice it and try to help, too. Though often one recommendation may contradict another, everyone will say something clever, advising what one should do to correct this or alter that. Even though this may be a bit chaotic the dancer tries out all the suggestions but, understandably, not always with success. Then others may propose different solutions or may look for, and find, other faults in the dancer's technique such as problems of co-ordination, rhythm, breathing, focusing, turn-out, turn-in, body weight, height, stamina, pull-up, etc.; they will all come up in due course. Every possible weakness will be discovered, magnified and diagnosed as the possible cause of the failure in question. The dancer who, a few days ago, was apt, talented and promising with just one temporary technical problem, is suddenly made aware of a magnitude of inadequacies in basic technique.

Though artists normally welcome technical challenges – which make work more interesting and enhance one's progress – the present situation doesn't exactly boost the dancer's morale, and that is only half the trouble. The most disturbing part is that the more corrections one receives, the more mixed-up and nervous one becomes. Tension builds up to such an extent that instead of achieving better control the muscles become tired and co-ordination fails. Trying to follow so much varied advice simultaneously causes an inability to focus on the real issue in question and, through over-practice, physical and mental exhaustion will follow.

The dancer will think along these lines: 'What on earth is the matter with me? Not only do I possess a faulty technique and lack talent, I must be crazy too! I am privileged to have highly skilled professionals helping me. Anyone else in my shoes would make great progress, but what do I do? I'm falling to pieces.

'Others would calm down on hearing comforting words like: "Sooner or later every dancer goes through a similar crisis, don't overdramatise things, you are neither unique nor more insane than the rest of us." But what do I do? I become even more impatient with myself.

'If everyone else can get over these problems, why can't I? The other dancers relax when hearing encouraging remarks: "There is nothing really wrong with you, it is just psychological," "You are getting this kind of blackout because you are all nerves," "It is only a question of correct co-ordination, but you can't do so because you are so tense," or "It is just a matter of correct breathing." But what do I do? I'm getting more and more frustrated. . .

'I should relax – but how? I should co-ordinate better – but how? I should breathe properly – but how? Actually, why don't I know how? I was told only what I am doing *wrong* but why am I not told *how* to do things *right?*'

By now the original problem – how to overcome a challenging technical hurdle – is overshadowed by all these torturing riddles. It takes many sleepless nights to find one's way out of this mental maze and considerably longer before discovering some answers to all these burning questions. In retrospect one realises how important it is for teachers to analyse such a complex situation, that may emerge both in professional life and in our daily teaching at all levels.

Technical faults and problems can be approached and successfully solved in different ways, but receiving so many varied corrections within a short period of time and trying to incorporate these suggestions could result in confusion. This may lead to a state of desperation in the dancer, whether professional or student. Many youngsters often find themselves in this vulnerable mental state, specially after attending certain types of Easter and Summer courses or, perhaps, while studying at a school where the same subject is taught to the same class in rota by several teachers. No matter how expert these pedagogues may be, their different approach to solving technical problems or diagnosing and correcting faults can often confuse the pupils.

Without being aware of it, we teachers may also cause frustration, panic and loss of self-confidence when we comment on faults in such general statements as: 'You can't co-ordinate if you are tense,' 'You must relax,' 'It is just psychological, just nerves,' or we console: 'Every dancer goes through a similar crisis,' or scold and criticise: 'Don't overdramatise,' 'You are not unique.' Criticising our students, telling them off or comforting them is sometimes unavoidable and necessary, but we need to give them distinct corrections, explicit advice and instructions for how to get over their physical and mental problems, otherwise we will only add to their confusion, reinforce their mental blocks and increase their desperation.

Those old faults

When I was a young dancer I had a teacher who gave excellently constructed company classes with *enchaînements* which were both artistic and demanding, but he hardly ever gave us personal corrections. We thought he probably didn't notice that this omission from our daily practice led to a feeling of insecurity and frustration, particularly for the younger members of the company.

One day we summoned up enough courage to mention this issue to him. To our surprise he said, 'If dancers at your level don't know enough about your skill and art, strength and shortcomings, to be able to make the most of a daily class, it's just too bad, and much too late. I'd be wasting precious practice time trying to correct what should have been put right during your student years. My duty is to construct classes correctly from a health point of view and, at the same time, to make them challenging and artistic. Your job is to follow them as best you can while using the exercises for your own advantage.'

His conviction seemed very strange, detached and unhelpful to us as our previous teachers had had exactly the opposite attitude. With the egotism of youngsters we didn't consider the possibility that at least some of his ideas might make sense. Most of us thought he was simply creating a theory in order to hide the fact that he hadn't any interest in teaching or understanding for corrections. As for myself – already involved with teaching – I took a solemn oath never to follow his example!

Later in my teaching career I often found it necessary to adapt or make changes to some of the principal ideas of teaching which I had learned, picked up over the years by experience and observation, or invented myself. However, one of the basic rules remained unchanged. I was convinced – as the majority of our profession was – that one of the most important tasks of a teacher was to watch like a hawk for dancers' faults. When shortcomings were noticed, corrections had to be given immediately and repeatedly before they became habit-forming.

This principle seemed indisputable and most straightforward: in an ideal world, all teachers should be able to find every single fault in each student's work, but years of experience have taught me that in practice this doesn't work without creating other problems.

In their early stages of training students often already have, or develop, some basic faults, specially if their yet-untrained bodies have not enough natural pliability to cope with the required technique. These shortcomings usually manifest themselves in unmistakable signs and will be immediately spotted, and corrected, by the teachers. However, an almost invisible misplacement of some part of the body, a slight and wrongly-shifted balance-line, or incorrect breathing, may pass unnoticed for long enough for it to become a lasting bad habit. These may easily undermine the precise execution of more advanced technical tasks in later years, furthermore they could lead to injuries, (I have discussed and demonstrated some of these problems in my video *Faults, Corrections and Perfections.*)

Seldom during the vocational school period do students study with only one teacher. Thus, as a rule, a student's obvious faults will be picked out and corrected by several teachers. This procedure may have the required good result but, in numerous cases and depending on the individual's character, it might have just the opposite effect.

The more sensitive pupils may find constant reminders of their faults from many of the staff to be depressing, irritating and even intimidating. Instead of trying to put the corrections into operation for a lasting cure they will lose self-confidence, become angry with themselves and develop complexes.

Some of the tougher students (especially the boys) might put on an attitude of self-defence, trying to take this 'nagging, hammering-it-in' attitude not too seriously until it becomes an almost familiar routine in their studies. Not only do they accept this procedure as normal, they get used to it, or even come to rely on these reminders of their inadequacies. Unconsciously they take it for granted that it is good enough if they correct their faults at the moment when they are told to do so, then they can forget them until the next time they are corrected again: one day it will all come together!

Other students may find excuses. They will persuade parents, school counsellors and themselves that they are unjustly penalised because of being disliked, a teacher's impatient attitude or a personality clash.

Whatever the case, all the above-mentioned problematic issues result in negative attitudes. The student will end up feeling angry, depressed and victimised, and may even develop a cynical 'who cares?' outlook. Some may become apathetic and build an 'immunising' defence against the irritating repetition of criticism – a temporary 'deafness' towards corrections. Under these circumstances the faults cannot be corrected for the better.

Unless teachers dismiss these students (seldom the case) their attention is directed to giving the same corrections repeatedly to the same student for the same, easily-detectable faults. Understandably, whether the teacher responds with patience or reacts with anger, this annoying and frustrating function makes their eyes tired and blind to the hidden faults which probably are causing the ones which they keep on correcting.

The situation may alter for the better if a student changes school, or is moved to study under different teachers in the same school who may have fresh visions. However, even in new circumstances, the 'old' faults and mannerisms will soon be discovered and instantly criticised. Even if the differing personality of the new teacher changes the pupil's response to a more positive direction, the constant mentioning of the same faults – although in a different manner – will further aggravate the student's existing complexes. This may again lead some youngster to desperation, a total loss of self-confidence and finally to an *idée fixe* that 'those old faults' are just not correctable.

When teaching in companies, one realises how the 'vicious circle' keeps weaving around the dancers. The longer the bad habits exist, the harder it is to get rid of them, and there comes a time when it seems to be too late.

Unless we teachers realise how many psychological problems we create, unintentionally, by correcting 'those old faults in those old ways' many dancers will carry with them throughout their entire careers their basic faults and the physical and mental injuries they may cause.

Great patience as well as imagination and inventiveness is needed to find different and varied approaches which would work for each individual. Teaching more movement analysis, involving the students' minds in becoming more self-confident, independent and able to do self-correction, changing the usual routine of correction by using different wording and speech tone, all these are potent parts of a successful modus operandi but they are not quite enough, and in the typical cases already mentioned one should consider additional teaching techniques.

When analysing human movement – and a dancer's technical shortcomings – one can approach and explain them from several angles. Instead of calling the dancer's attention constantly to the dreaded 'old fault' perhaps one should try to divert their concentration to a seemingly different but connected fault (like breathing, musicality, expression). Trying to put in order the new defect, and letting them forget the 'old' fault, often relaxes a dancer's mind from the idea-fixation, and corrects it subconsciously.

Hammering it in

A colleague brought a student of hers to one of my open classes. 'I want her to audition for the Royal Ballet Senior School, but first I would like her to have a couple of private lessons with you. I think she is very promising, but I might be biased as she's been studying with me for over five years. She's conscientious, has personality, elevation, turn-out and high extensions, but her *pirouettes*. . . We've tried simply everything, but they are still not up to standard, and she's got this irritating habit of lifting her shoulders. Please would you see if you can help?'

Indeed, the girl danced quite beautifully in the open class, though from time to time she tensed and lifted her shoulders a bit, and not only when turning. When it came to the pirouettes – no matter whether they were on or off *pointe, en dehors,* or *en dedans* – this fault was prominent and she failed to execute them properly. Each time she prepared for them she showed anxiety, her whole body became rigid with her shoulders up to her ears, her cheeks glowed red and the otherwise natural smile on her face froze into a mask-like grin.

If she was in such a state only at a stage of preparation it wasn't at all surprising that during the actual turns her neck became stiff, thus the head-spotting was too slow; because of her shoulders lifting she couldn't control her arm movements through the torso muscles; therefore they were moving in a clumsy and unhelpful manner. As for her breathing. . . it hindered more than helped her efforts!

First, I wanted to establish the few existing good points in her *pirouette* technique – a proper balance-line, correct placement of the pelvis and good use of her turn-out. This appreciation cheered her up and obviously gave her some hope. To keep up her good spirits and not destroy her self-confidence, I decided not to shower her with the complete list of her bad habits but to tackle them one at a time.

I wished to give priority to the 'lifted shoulders' issue as it was such an eyesore. Secretly, I hoped that in correcting this fault a few other problems would be cleared away, too, which might lead us eventually to find the cause of her faulty *pirouettes*. If this were to happen there would be no need to waste any further time and upset her positive mood by 'rubbing in' all her mistakes (which probably existed only as a result of the basic fault).

As soon as I mentioned the word 'shoulders' she reacted nervously, 'Oh, I know about that. My teacher has been correcting it ever since I did my first *pirouette*. She must think me stupid. I can't understand why I am unable to discipline myself more and just get rid of this awful thing!'

'Maybe you are relying on your teacher's constant corrections too much and adjusting your fault only after she has finished criticising you instead of trying to think ahead.'

'In the past I was guilty of dancing without thinking and leaving corrections to my teacher, but lately – believe me – this isn't the case. She's changed her 'tactics' too. Nowadays she tries to prevent me from doing things wrong by giving me warnings about my shoulders ahead of the action. Instead of correcting me while I am doing the *pirouette*, or after I have committed the fault, she always calls my attention to it during the preparation. So I have a chance to think about it again just a few seconds later while I am actually performing the turn. It really should work, shouldn't it? But in fact it makes me so nervous that it becomes worse!' By this time she was trying to fight back her tears. 'My stupid 'lifted' shoulders stop me from having good *pirouettes*.'

'I am not so sure about that. Up to a certain point it does hinder your turning technique and, of course, it isn't a pretty sight either, which is another good reason to correct it. The truth is that there are many dancers who lift their shoulders higher than ballet aesthetics allow but they still manage to execute adequate *pirouettes*. It may be an eyesore but this is not the real cause of the problem.'

'Really?' Though she looked doubtful, her tears stopped tricking down her cheeks.

'I'm not saying this just to comfort you. Let's forget your 'idea-fixation' about your shoulders for a while and try to find the real target.'

In order to calm her I decided that I wouldn't mention the word 'shoulders' again and started to concentrate on her *pirouette* preparations. I asked her to remember always to relax, breathe out, and keep very still for a few seconds whilst in the preparatory *demi-plié*.

Breathing out before starting the *pirouette* made her shoulders relax into their natural place without her even thinking of them so, at the right moment, her arms were also at the required height.

Next she had to learn that, when she was breathing out, she must use her back and neck muscles simultaneously in such a way that she could drop her shoulder-blades and lock them down at the same time. Now she must practise keeping this locked position firm while breathing in and holding her breath during the *pirouette*. Soon, the 'lifted shoulder' symptom began to disappear from her turns. As soon as this was accomplished it was easy for her to understand how to apply this correct muscle control of her torso, combined with the right breathing, to the rest of her work. In addition, having learnt to empty her lungs at the time of the preparation, she was able to breathe in properly and supply her muscles with fresh oxygen at the moment when she needed the strength to perform the *pirouette*. Soon her *pirouettes* became well polished, reliable and strong with her shoulders and arms in a graceful position.

The short time in which she was able to correct so many of her long-time problems surprised me because she was only an inexperienced student and, even for professionals, it always took much longer to correct habitual faults than to learn something from scratch.

Her rapid progress couldn't be explained by either the purely physical interference of making use of so-far uncontrolled neck and back muscles and correct respiration, or that this student had talent and intelligence. All these components were essential for success but there must have been other helpful factors which perhaps were not of a physical nature. I was determined to seek them in order to use them in the future.

My colleague came to see our final private lesson. I don't know which of us was the happiest when the girl 'showed off' her achievements. As we watched quite a few satisfactory *pirouettes* my colleague whispered, 'You've got her *pirouettes* but how on earth did you get rid of those lifted shoulders?'

'I directed her concentration towards using the muscles at the top of her torso, and to her breathing correctly. I deliberately ignored the 'shoulder complex'.'

'Did I 'hammer it in' too much?'

Suddenly it struck me that the combination of our thoughts might just have given me the answer to my question in a nutshell: correcting a fault repeatedly over too long a time and in the same manner may become the cause of long-lasting complexes. Approaching the problem from a different direction gave us the solution.

Say cheeeese. . .!

When I was about nine years old I went to a children's camp for my summer holidays. It would have been a perfect vacation except for one thing: I desperately missed my dance classes. However, I soon noticed all over the resort posters advertising 'talent-spotting' dance auditions for the following weekend to be held at a nearby theatre. These would be followed by a few weeks of study with a 'world-famous' former ballerina and the course would culminate in some public performances.

According to the posters this project was the 'opportunity of a lifetime' and 'the gateway to FAME'. The conditions seemed simple, too: one had to be of a reasonable age (whatever that might mean, the limits were not mentioned!), and the fees for the audition, tuition and costume-hire were to be paid in advance (these expenses also remained a mystery since no actual sum was indicated).

The age limitation didn't worry me as I couldn't imagine that at the advanced age of nine I might be considered too young; as far as the fees were concerned, I childishly believed that my pocket money would easily settle the matter. In fact this seemed to me to be a worthwhile investment rather than a sacrifice. I imagined that I had a strong chance of becoming a 'discovery' since the torturing feeling of self-doubt was still unknown to me then.

All I needed was my mother's permission which I hoped to gain when she visited me at the weekend. However, after reading the information on the poster, her immediate reaction was absolutely negative. She tried to reason with me but, realising that I was too young to understand her point of view and that I would be heart-broken, she let herself be persuaded to take me along so we could find out more about this 'unique' project before she made her final decision.

When we arrived at the gloomy, neglected theatre there were already waiting many candidates from all the holiday camps in the surrounding area. We were all shapes, sizes and ages (from three to thirty!). To my surprise hardly anyone was dressed properly for a class, and to my mother's horror even some of the youngest girls were already wearing make-up, dressed in tasteless costumes and with ridiculously elaborate hair-dos in the style of Hollywood child stars.

I felt uncomfortable and insecure. I didn't know whether to admire or hate this strange set-up. For the first time in my 'professional life' I began to doubt if my chosen vocation was the right one.

'Let's go,' whispered my mother, 'you can see for yourself that this isn't your scene.' Although I was already losing confidence I still couldn't give up my dreams as easily as that. I hesitated. 'Surely,' she continued, 'you don't wish to be turned into a little monkey like these miserable mites!' I was almost won over when the candidates were suddenly called to line up. In a split second I tore away from my mother to find myself face-to-face with the 'world-famous' ballerina.

She looked anything but what I had imagined a celebrated dance personality should look like. I expected someone just a bit older than my own teacher – whom I idolised – with all her charm and grace, and more if it was possible. Instead, I saw a pitiful, grotesque-looking creature in front of me.

Her face was covered in thick layers of greasepaint and an insincere smile froze on her mouth in an unsuccessful attempt to disguise her age and unpleasant features. But then, this mask-like make-up might be a shield behind which she could observe us without revealing her true personality. She was dressed in garments of loud and vulgar colours which were too tightly fitting, quite unsuitable for her ageing figure. Her hands with fingernails covered in blood-coloured varnish appeared aggressive, and her orange-red tinted hair looked repulsive and was styled in an absurdly embellished manner. She smelt of stale tobacco, brandy and a nauseous, sweet perfume. Her voice was shrill and high-pitched, and her movements without any grace. There was absolutely nothing to like, respect or admire in this hideous woman.

She taught us a few steps and enchaînements which were accompanied by some hardly audible music – played by a 'bored-to-death' pianist on an out-of-tune piano. While we practised our steps the teacher constantly banged on the floor with a stick and shouted: 'Keep smiling my angels; say cheese; show your teeth; nobody died, give us a smile, darling!' It was as if nothing else mattered in this audition except smiling.

I felt perfectly miserable but I tried to follow her orders, but the more she said it the less I could bring myself to smile. While my facial muscles froze into some sort of grin, my body and mind became so tense that I was hardy able to move or remember the order of the steps. Disappointment, disillusion and despair built up inside me and I began to cry.

'Sweetie-pie, I didn't instruct you to cry, but to smile!' Her honey-coated mocking made some of the children giggle and I felt ridiculed. 'But of course it's not your fault, my dearie, that your teacher didn't teach you always to smile while you dance.'

That was too much! I couldn't bear to hear her discrediting my teacher. Anger stopped the flow of tears as I riposted: 'My teacher doesn't need to command us to smile. Studying with her is so wonderful that it just happens, without instructions.'

That is how I lost both my chance and interest to be 'discovered' at the age of nine!

This episode happened a very long time ago and even then it was an extreme case from every point of view. Fortunately, the type of teacher I have just described hardly exists now but, unfortunately, the theory of 'compulsive smiling' and its bad effects are still with us to a certain extent.

It is not unusual to see in classes, as well as rehearsals – particularly when there is no specific dramatic message to convey – some dancers moving with either strained or blank faces. To remind them to smile might seem the simplest (and quickest) remedy.

However, when a smile is produced 'to order' rather than coming naturally from the artist's emotions it lasts for only a short while or, if it does remain, it will become an empty, doll-like grin. To remind constantly dancers to smile can also make them nervous and inhibited and – specially in the case of youngsters – might disturb their concentration.

Perhaps it is not 'The Smile' which one should be after but spirited dancing in which the joy of movement will manifest itself instinctively in the face.

If lack of talent is not the cause of uninspired dancing then it could be due to some physical or mental stress which may stem from the way the teacher conducts classes and rehearsals, but it could also be due to other psychological problems. Whatever the case it should be investigated, with the assistance of an expert if needed.

Dance students and dancers dance because of their love for the art. When the physical or psychological roots of their problems are cured they will instinctively move in a spirited and expressive manner without needing to be nagged about a 'compulsory smile'.

❖

Constructive Corrections

Modus operandi

I was a guest teacher with a well-known ballet company when I was approached by the director of the company's school to give a couple of ballet classes to her students.

The director and her staff watched these lessons which were followed by the usual lunch and informal professional chit-chat. We compared both differences and similarities of our work and ideas. Questions and answers flowed back and forth. I was quite impressed by the standards of the students and expressed this with sincerity.

However, the fairly young teacher who was in charge of the graduates said, 'It is generous of you to compliment the work of my students but I wasn't satisfied with the way they performed in your classes at all. I don't know whether to be ashamed or angry. I loved watching you as you taught something which was new to the class, but when I heard you give basically the same corrections that I give every day, I was terribly disappointed. I couldn't even feel any satisfaction that you kept finding the same faults in style and technique as I did. It made me so cross to see how some of these girls reacted. Today they seemed to be hearing these criticisms for the very first time when they should be tired of hearing them from me so often!'

'I am sure that it was excitement and nervous tension which made them repeat some of their old faults when working with a strange master,' said another member of staff.

'One always notices more faults when watching another teacher working with one's own students,' remarked an older colleague.

'Well, it looks to me as though these girls don't pay enough attention to my words. I just hope that hearing them from you, at least, will make a lasting impression on them,' commented the graduates' teacher.

I felt that I had to say something 'comforting and clever' but I was aware of the dangers of sounding patronising – the last thing I wanted to be. With some embarrassment I said something like, 'This is a very usual symptom which happens to all of us in these circumstances. Students often become a bit 'deaf' to their regular teacher's voice after a while, just as children often ignore their parents' warnings, and we teachers may become temporarily 'blind' to our regular pupils' faults, as parents often do with their offspring. Naturally, teachers of the same subject more or less teach and correct in the same way but, because we all have varying personalities, some of us may get through better to particular individuals and impress or influence them more than others.'

'This is exactly why I always ask guests to give us a few classes,' explained the director. 'I find it is beneficial to the students, and refreshing for the teachers. Another voice, a differing accent, or just a change of wording with the same meaning – and the occasional new approach – might alter the students' comprehension and reaction. All these factors can act as an eye-opener to the resident staff, too. The result should be reassuring for most of the time but, even if it isn't, it might make one 're-think' what one is doing or, rather, not doing correctly. In any case it might have some effect on everyone involved, like a kind of 'blood-transfusion'.'

I was relieved to hear these wise words because it wasn't for the first time that directors and resident teachers have reacted with the same sense of disappointed surprise when watching their own pupils being taught by an 'outsider' at summer courses, seminars or congresses. They often behave as though they were on trial and need to explain that it is the students' carelessness or tension, and not their own incompetence, which has created a situation where the guest teacher may find 'uncorrected' faults in the students' work. Why does this almost resentful fear and negative, self-destructive reaction exist, rather than the acceptance of a process which is inevitable and natural, and has numerous positive consequences?

In the world of dancing the 'invited' teachers act a vitally important part, as some pollinating insects do for plants in nature. They bring to the resident teachers in companies and schools the 'fertilising pollen' in the form of fresh ideas without which our art could not survive. At the same time the 'guests' feed on the 'nectar' received from the 'hosts' – teacher and student – by way of seeing and learning from the results, good and mediocre, and by trying to be more flexible in adapting methods that suit the particular circumstances at each new place of work. Such new experiences should widen their own horizons and prevent narrow-minded stagnation.

There are even more facts to be considered. It seems that 'teacher's blindness', which may develop as a result of daily routine, is quite a common disease and it is also apparent that students easily become temporarily 'deaf' to their accustomed teacher's corrections and praise. To some degree such symptoms are due to human nature and will occur from time to time. However, there are students who are more 'deaf' to some teachers than they are to others – and for longer periods of time.

What are the reasons behind this problem and can they be changed for the better? Is it always due to the inattentiveness of some students or is it an indication of how good or bad a teacher's communication is? Is he or she capable of gaining the students' interest, concentration and complete trust and creating an atmosphere in which corrections can be made effective?

The art of teaching needs not only special talents and a wide knowledge but also a highly-refined technique of teaching. Perhaps some students' 'deafness' and teachers' 'blindness' may be caused by the lack or inadequacy of such teaching techniques.

Teachers, when starting their careers, naturally follow their own teacher's path in 'what' and 'how' they convey and correct. As years of teaching experience go by and their personality matures, they may well add to these traditions some of their own ideas as well as developing a personal teaching skill through which they achieve their best results. For certain recurring faults the teacher will have the same corrections delivered in the same manner, probably spoken in the same words, emphasised with the same tonality. Though this method has proved naturally to lead to a fruitful outcome, in many cases the repetitive, unchanging manner might fossilise the procedure and could become the cause of 'blindness' and 'deafness'.

We teachers cannot escape from our personal traits – nor should we attempt to do so – or change our convictions about how to achieve high standards with our pupils: but we should continuously search for a great variety of approaches for each issue we wish to convey and correct. This is an essential part of the *modus operandi*.

Psychological detours

After a *Sleeping Beauty* performance the Blue Bird – a principal dancer whose class-room work I knew to be impeccable and of a virtuoso standard – complained to me bitterly, 'Ever since I was a student my teachers kept telling me that I wasn't strong enough for virtuoso roles. To prove them wrong I've worked harder than any of my colleagues. Now I am a principal, dancing a technically demanding role which should be utterly air-bound,' he mimicked the flight of a bird, 'but each time I dance it I am more earthbound than ever! Towards the end of the variation I feel tired and unable to control those *entrechats* six and the *sissonnes en tournant*. I can't make them look as light and carefree as the flight of a bird. . .! It seems ridiculous that in rehearsals I have more than enough strength to dance the entire part over and over again, but on stage it is beyond my powers to perform it just once without feeling exhausted. It's frustrating. Why is this happening to me?'

I ventured to find some suitable explanation. 'Most dancers use up more energy during a performance than they do in rehearsal. They get additional strength from being in an ecstatic state of mind by performing on stage. However, serious physical pain or mental worry may easily suppress that supply of extra energy and lead to exhaustion. Are you injured or, perhaps, worried about something?'

'I've no physical injuries but the fear of not being strong enough is always in my mind. I keep hearing the voices of my teachers as they kept 'hammering' it in, "You're too weak", "You must work harder", "You'll never make it." Were they right? Can you help me to get more technique and to build up more strength?'

'If that's what you want we can start tomorrow after rehearsals,' I answered to calm him. In reality, I had no idea how I could serve such an excellent dancer with no apparent failings and more than enough technique and stamina to excel on stage.

I realised that at this point I couldn't help by simply telling him that he is just suffering from a 'weakness' complex and that overworking would be senseless and harmful. The only way I could assist him to perform successfully in the future would be to make him forget his 'idea-fixation'. I decided that during the coaching sessions I should take his strength for granted and not even mention such words as 'technique' and 'stamina'.

I decided to direct his attention to completely different problems which were equally important.

My first approach was to make him concentrate on his

breathing. When he was on stage and in an anxious state of mind his respiration was heavy, uneven and inefficient. I thought that to analyse in minute detail his variation and coda, from this angle, could have beneficial effects. Learning how to control the oxygen supply and use it to the best advantage would save him much wasted energy. Once he improved his breathing technique he wouldn't feel so tired and this would help him to dance with self-confidence – and brilliance.

I also suggested that we should re-analyse the choreography from the point of view of the bird-like movements, so that he could emphasise these characteristics more effectively. The combination of an improved respiration technique and artistic expression gave him enough new stimuli to make him think of the role very differently.

His interpretation soon changed, 'I am dancing this role now with real joy! Instead of struggling to imitate a bird's flight I can make myself believe that I am actually flying.' And so did the audience when he next performed the role.

For the first night of a new production of *Don Quixote* a guest choreographer wanted to cast a young ballerina in the role of Kitri. From every point of view she was absolutely right for the part – except for her speed. The company's ballet master was quick to remind her, 'Well, well. Those speedy variations and codas are going to be devilishly difficult for you, my dear. You'll have to work day and night and harder than anybody else in order to prove that you are not miscast!'

After eight weeks of frantic, panic-stricken rehearsals – conducted day and night by the foreign choreographer's personal assistant, with the help of an interpreter and one of the company's répétiteurs – she showed great promise in style, presentation and characterisation. As far as technical matters were concerned she was also coming quite close to the standards required except for, as forecast, some of the very *fast enchaînements*, particularly those in the first act.

At the end of her first stage rehearsal I found her in the dressing-room as white as a sheet. She was trembling from fatigue and fright, and crying bitterly. All pleading with the foreign coach to allow her to dance some parts just a little more slowly was in vain. She turned to me, 'I am as slow as a snail, and I should be as fast as quicksilver. It'll be a disaster, I'll never be able to cope with these speeds.'

'In the past you may have had some difficulty in moving fast, but watching your *allegro* work recently in class, and in rehearsal today, I am satisfied that you have all the speed you really need. You could overcome the problem easily if you would time and emphasise some of the movements slightly differently within a musical phrase.'

'What do you mean?'

We went through the critical parts of the ballet just from the musical point of view. I forced her concentration into a new direction by making her find the numerous places in the choreography where she could save a few split seconds and feel more comfortable while dancing.

We discovered how often she over-emphasised some of the less important parts of the 'linking' or 'preparatory' steps – thereby wasting precious time. I proved to her that, besides enhancing the artistic quality, lots of tiny bits of extra time could be gained by making the right use of the musical upbeat and anticipating better the more difficult movements.

To concentrate on these many nuances meant a study of the technical part of the entire role from a completely different angle. It was mentally demanding and left her no time for panic. With each additional rehearsal she achieved better speed and facility. Now she could spare strength and concentrate more on the characterisation of this demanding role. Two weeks later she danced brilliantly at the premiere.

Because of over-repetitive corrections in the past, a dancer's knowledge of individual technical deficiencies and faults may become embedded in the sub-conscious. This can cause severe setbacks during a dancer's career. Yet, by tactfully using a few 'psychological detours', one can easily lead these artists back to true form.

Tricking the mind

A talented young dancer requested from me a series of private lessons in order to help her in a specific problem: 'I am constantly criticised by the company teachers for being too light on my feet. I don't seem to use either the power or the protective quality of the *demi-plié* in my dancing. Because of my feeble *pliés* and *fondus*, my *pirouettes* and *ronds de jambe fouettés* are also suffering. Though I have no real problems with very fast technique, and elevation also comes easily, I keep getting injuries.'

'Did you ever have any trouble with your Achilles tendons?'

'Never. Moreover, I was told that they are sufficiently long.'

'Have you had a recent injury?'

'Not really. It must be something else that is wrong. I have had this fault ever since I was a student. For years and years my teachers kept on correcting it. It was mentioned in all my reports, and I really tried hard to improve it but without much result. I should like to know whether there is something anatomically wrong with me, or am I simply misusing my muscles in some particular movements?'

'Perhaps it is the latter. Whatever the cause we must try to find a solution before your 'instrument' becomes injured again. Please show me a couple of your famous *demi-pliés* in each position.'

She executed the lot, but they weren't even average. All over her were obvious signs of tension. She suddenly had become the typical image of a dancer struggling under psychological stress. She was overworking unnecessarily, doing all the things which would surely hinder rather than help her efforts. Her whole physique became rigid, she held in her breath, her otherwise delicate arms and hands were strained to such an extent that her fingers were spiky and slightly trembling. She stiffened her neck so much that her veins bulged. The thigh muscles tightened and bunched up instead of elongating softly. To complete this sad but familiar picture the infamous 'ballet smile' was switched on automatically and set in a frozen position on her pretty face.

'What are your major concerns while you are doing your *pliés?*'

'I'm concentrating mainly on pulling up my torso so I don't weigh too heavily over the bending knees. At the same time, I am trying to push down and deepen the *plié* without arching my back or rolling my feet. These are the principles I was taught.'

'Rightly so!'

'It seems that I have the correct ideas as well as the facility, but I still can't get it right! Am I not using my brain or my muscles enough?'

'Hmmm. . . Probably you are doing too 'much' with both. Anyway, let's consider this whole procedure differently and in a more relaxed way. For a little while just forget about that 'pulling up', and especially about the 'pushing down' business. As a professional you can take it for granted that when *pliéing* you will automatically pull up your torso – as indeed you do – and that you'd bend the knees to your limit. Instead of concentrating on

lifting up the top or pressing down from the legs, try to think of
your knees as if they have a life of their own and want to escape
from each other. Don't work hard, let it happen. Enlarging the gap
between one's knees, while keeping the feet in the required turned-
out position with a very smooth, flowing muscle-tone, should feel
the most natural task for a classically trained dancer.'

'Oh, it is so much easier this way! Are my *demi-pliés* really
deeper than before?'

'Yes. Earlier, you overworked and under-achieved, and looked
uneasy. Not only have you done them much better now,
you've reached a better-than-average depth in a relaxed and most
pleasing way. Let's do some *fondus* with a similar approach.'
Considering it was her first attempt at *fondus* using this different
method, she performed them with very promising results again.

Afterwards it took us a lot of patient and concentrated work in
the class-room to stabilise the good results and to make an
effective use on stage of her newly achieved, deeper and more
powerful *demi-pliés* and *fondus* in elevation, *pirouettes, pointe-
work* and *adage*.

After a few successful performances she said, 'I'm still puzzled
about why for years I couldn't get the 'secret' of *demi-pliés* if there
was nothing anatomically wrong with my body? What 'magic'
was needed to help me understand how to perform some basic
technical tasks which I couldn't do correctly during my entire
professional training?'

'I think your brain was playing a little trick on you. It often
happens. Though our mind sometimes understands a given
problem quite clearly, and knows the right answer, under physical
stress – perhaps trying to overcome pain caused by injury – or
nervous tension – being constantly reminded of a specific fault, as
in your case – the brain keeps sending to most parts of the body
'alerting' messages which temporarily create over-tense muscles.
Without having the right balance between tension and relaxation,
the body is incapable of producing the required movements with
the right quality. Under nervous pressure it may happen that the
brain sends its messages either too late or too early, sometimes
even to the wrong part of the body.

'For a long time you were constantly told that your *demi-pliés*
and *fondus* were inadequate. Naturally, this always made you
anxious when you were performing these movements. Probably
your brain knew perfectly well that to achieve the natural
characteristics of these basic exercises you needed to use the

'melting' type of muscle-tone but, because you were too anxious to get it right, your brain might have kept on sending the wrong messages – to strain those muscles which should have relaxed. Being in a nervous state of mind, you were also breathing incorrectly, which made your muscles even more tense and cramped.

'In such cases one should try to 'fool' one's brain! What I tried to teach you was how to approach an acute problem differently from an already outworn and irritating way. I expected that your brain wouldn't recognise it as being familiar and therefore might respond and adjust to the re-packaged complex with fresh interest as though it was an entirely new one.'

Of course, there was the possibility that her brain might have recognised immediately that the old and annoying problem was just 'dressed in a new frock'. However, whatever the case, we couldn't fail. Every healthy mind – particularly those of a young and ambitious artist – will always embrace sensible ideas and new methods, indeed this is the key to human progress.

Whether I had succeeded in really 'tricking her mind' or just giving her new hope through focusing her attention differently and re-grouping her thoughts, was not important. There had not been any 'magic', only a *modus operandi* which created a relaxed, optimistic atmosphere. Such circumstances, free of anxiety, were a guarantee for more precision in concentration, correction and 're-learning'. They seemed to solve for this young dancer – as for many others before her – a long-lasting and depressing fight over an acute and destructive situation.

❖

Practical Solutions for More Efficiency

Teaching to learn

In some articles published in *The Dancing Times* and lectures given at various conferences I have been arguing the case that professional students should be taught to practise their art with a self-conscious and analytical approach to help them detect and correct their own faults. These arguments have met with a favourable response from several colleagues but some doubts have been raised about their practicality. Several problems were mentioned: 'Teaching pupils to recognise their shortcomings and to find solutions for them on their own would need much more extra teaching time,' 'Many of these youngsters will probably be bored practising in this manner,' 'To make students think more while dancing might result in diminished concentration on their dancing. It could interrupt the rhythm, speed and continuous flow of movements which are so necessary for a well-balanced class,' 'Few schools have regular coaching sessions as part of the timetable and there is hardly enough time in daily classes to convey and polish the subject matter to the required standards. How can one possibly fit in this extra work?'

Indeed, private lessons and coaching sessions provide obvious opportunities for such an approach. However, one might find other possibilities or create such circumstances within the daily practice so that both goals can be achieved at the same time without interrupting the chain of physical activity during class or rehearsals.

One day, during a professional class, I noticed that a certain young soloist who was a bit of a workaholic was practising very below her usual standard.

'Forgive me, I am feeling quite unwell.'

She certainly looked very ill. 'You'd better pack up and go home to bed.'

'I would like to continue gently please, I have some important rehearsals later.'

'I wouldn't continue class if I were you, but if you want to kill time until the rehearsal why don't you just watch for once?'

'Oh, I hate watching others dancing instead of doing it myself. It makes me jealous and frustrated.'

Her attitude didn't surprise me as I was familiar with most dancers' and students' negative opinions on this matter. Seeing how unwell she was I spared her a lecture about how useful it is to observe daily practice occasionally; nevertheless, I remarked, 'It might help to divert your thoughts from feeling so ill.'

She gave in and sat down. During the class I continued to raise her interest. Sometimes I called her attention to watch how a minute detail of a dancer's individual approach, such as a slightly altered breathing, timing of a movement or power distribution, could change, for better or worse, the execution of a certain exercise. I pointed out a couple of dancers for her to observe how the line or style of their movements was influenced by the correct, or incorrect, use of certain muscles. Gradually she became more and more involved, looking interested and definitely less under the weather.

As I corrected a dancer's shoulder position in a preparation for a *pirouette*, she suddenly exclaimed, 'Gosh! This is exactly what you told me the other day. I can see now so clearly what I was doing wrong but I couldn't quite put it right then. Looking from the outside it seems so simple to correct.'

Soon after this event I learnt that the girl had glandular fever, so I was greatly surprised when, after about a fortnight, she visited class.

'I'm terribly happy to see you here but shouldn't you be at home and resting, besides,' I said teasingly, 'I thought you felt jealous, angry and frustrated to watch?'

'I still do and in my present miserable situation more than ever, but I begin to see its benefits. When you focused my attention on certain points a completely new perspective opened up. I realised how much one can learn if one does it in the right way. Anyway, I would like to make good use of my convalescent period by coming to observe classes. I want to learn how to watch and listen better so I may see and hear more. *I want to learn how to learn!*'

Her response and proposal pleased me a lot not only because I hoped that our little scheme might act as an anti-depressant and tonic during her long and tiring time of recuperation but because

I guessed, as indeed it happened, that her future progress would be enhanced by these experiences. Later, when she was able to continue with her career, it was amazing to see how intelligently she applied to her own work many of the corrections in technique and style which she had observed, and probably analysed as well, during her rehabilitation.

She wasn't the only one who gained a lot from this situation; I learnt just as much as she did. I realised that in both professional and student classes, particularly the latter, I didn't need any more to put up with the presence of injured dancers sitting as passive onlookers somewhere behind my back, isolated from the lucky doers, looking but not seeing with their sleepy, vacant eyes, feeling forgotten, bored and depressed, and wasting their precious time. Furthermore, I became aware that this mutually demoralising situation – of ignored people compelled to watch class, and teachers trying to teach with enthusiasm while enduring the presence of uninterested dancers – is not necessarily the fault of the pupils.

It is possible to change these circumstances. We don't need private lessons, coaching sessions or the interruption of the flow of classes to teach our short- and long-term convalescing pupils how to approach technique more analytically, which would surely lead them to understand their own problems better and to correct them independently. Changing depression caused by inactivity into a new and useful interest proves to be a great help psychologically to a multitude of indisposed dancers. It also can save teachers from having to tolerate the ill effects caused by unresponsive, envious and embittered bystanders who (like wallflowers sitting it out at a ball), unwillingly influence the good atmosphere of energy-demanding and artistically-creative classes.

This example of analytical teaching doesn't act only as a tonic during periods of illness. During the many years of training and professional life a large number of dancers unavoidably become injured and ill, therefore most of them could be involved at some time in such experiences. This is one way through which one can lead students and dancers to recognise how their physical problems can be helped by using their minds.

When teaching at one of the vocational schools I was given an opportunity to teach extra tutorial lessons regularly to my graduate students after their daily classes. In these lessons I had four students each day. At these 'shared private lessons' I paid special attention to each student's individual technical problems but I made sure that the actual programme was determined by the pupils. At the beginning of each tutorial I asked them what specific technical task they wanted help with. If needed and asked for, I gave them corrective exercises for achieving such things as a better turn-out from the hips, or some special stretching exercises to help attain better placed and higher extensions without injury. Then we would work in turn on their requests with all four students taking part in each exercise.

During one of these tutorials I was called away to the principal's office. 'Continue, please,' I said, 'but only two at a time, while the other two watch. If the 'watchers' can spot any faults please give the proper corrections and make the 'doers' repeat the exercise correctly. Then, if I am not back by that time, please change roles.'

Ten minutes later I found the students working with each other so intensively that they didn't even notice my return. By now three of them were correcting the one who originally asked for help in this exercise. Their corrections, though given timidly, were quite valid. They corrected the obviously 'ugly' lines and gave such good advice as 'pull up', 'turn out more' or 'lift the leg higher', which all helped to a certain degree but didn't quite solve the key problem. After fully appreciating my students' first teaching efforts I asked the corrected pupil to repeat the step a few more times while I pointed out to the others what I thought the basic fault to be.

'Time to change the roles, please.'

Now, after fully understanding how to perform this step correctly and at the same time powerfully and gracefully, the girls were executing the exercise quite well, making use of the same corrections they had just given to their poor guinea-pig. She, enjoying a well-deserved rest, was eagerly watching and from her remarks it was obvious that she understood quite clearly what she had been doing wrong. There wasn't the slightest sign of impatience or boredom.

I sensed that these youngsters were very pleased to experience that wonderful feeling of satisfaction which occurs only when one strikes a perfect balance between successful physical and mental activity. This may even have been the first time that they fully appreciated that dancing is a combination of intense physical and mental activity.

It was a pleasant surprise to see how those students who were firmly set on an active dancing career became so interested and involved in an activity which appeared to be more teaching than performing: analysing, correcting and helping each other's faults. The news of this game-like tutorial spread fast and I was obliged to repeat it with the rest of my graduates in other tutorial groups. They became quite popular as they produced immediate good results. From that moment we worked in this way regularly and systematically, though for the time being only in our tutorial sessions. However, we soon realised that the method could be applied also very effectively in repertoire classes as most of the time these have to be divided into very small working groups, especially when practising solo variations.

Apart from the better technical achievements this correcting, helping-each-other method gradually brought about a healthy spirit of teamwork throughout all the other classes and rehearsals. This good atmosphere added an extra lift to the pupils' general progress and also gave them some natural protection from those stressful anxieties which often develop during the final few months of a student's life.

After a while I noticed that the graduate students didn't limit our game only to the 'privileged' tutorial and repertoire classes. They were often seen after class in studio corners and corridors, anywhere where they could work, correcting and helping each other in their *pirouettes*, extensions, *batteries*, balances, etc.

Some of these students were also involved in the school's choreographic activities. Now they found that, through being able to analyse a movement better, they could convey their own choreographic ideas faster and more precisely, especially if these were unconventional, invented images, and they could correct or help the performers execute the movements exactly as required.

Through this new approach to their work the students also began to understand and appreciate much better the difficult task of their teachers, and a few even thought about choosing this vocation for themselves if, or when, they are obliged to give up active dancing.

Realising they were beginning to think of a long-term future I also pointed out to them that good movement analysis is the foundation of a dance notator's job. Some students considered this to be another interesting possibility for the time to come.

Educating our pupils to help themselves more – by using their mental powers just as much as their physical ability – doesn't only mean producing better and more independent dancers. If some of our students, for one reason or another, cannot become dancers, it is comforting to know that we did not raise their hopes in vain but prepared them mentally for and attracted them to other dance-related careers.

I felt that all this was a promising start but it was still limited. Why should one teach in this beneficial way only at graduate level, and why just in privileged circumstances? It dawned on me that actually this might be the wrong way round anyway. Perhaps one should teach all vocational students in this more analytical and intellectually demanding manner throughout their studying years, within their daily classes, little by little, without any need of special coaching sessions or private lessons. One could easily adapt this method to the requirements and intelligence levels of the various age groups. By the time students reach their graduation year there would be hardly any necessity for corrective tutorials; rather this precious time, space and energy should be used for 'one to one' coaching focused on artistic quality and personal identity.

There are several ways by which one might make such an approach work successfully. One could make it part of the daily class routine in centre and diagonal exercises, when students are working in small groups, twos or individually. Those waiting could be asked to pay critical attention to those in action. A student in the waiting group could occasionally be requested to analyse the fault and correct it in front of the whole class and under the teacher's supervision. At other times the perpetrator of the fault can also be asked to make self-corrections. Another essential method could be to involve the injured or otherwise indisposed pupils in the same process.

Finally, and most importantly, we teachers should be the best example to our students in making sure that our corrections are analytical, directly to the point and non-generalising, clearly demonstrated physically, and spoken precisely and comprehensibly according to the age, gender and personality of the pupils. At the same time these should be intellectually challenging to involve the students' mental capacities to the utmost.

The illiterates

I was a young student when I first heard about dance notation – from Alice Turnay, a wonderful contemporary teacher. She had studied the Laban technique as well as Labanotation and believed enthusiastically in the importance of dancers being able accurately to record and read their own art. She explained to us that dance notation should serve a dancer or choreographer in the same way as the written word does a poet, novelist and dramatist, and music notation does to a composer, conductor, musician and singer – something that is concisely and precisely written down so that it may be read and reinterpreted with accuracy.

She said, 'Without making use of a notation of their own – as far as their art was concerned – dancers will remain simply 'illiterates'! Accurate dance notation is the scientific backbone of our art.' This impressed me no end because it sounded very cerebral, although at the time I didn't quite understand what she meant. As I respected and trusted her opinions fully, it seemed logical that I should study dance notation although this subject was not on the timetable.

My teacher agreed to instruct me after school hours but, after a couple of lessons, the horrors of the Second World War put an end to these studies. Afraid of Nazi persecution, she fled from Hungary and, to my great sadness, I never discovered if she survived. After this traumatic experience and other disruptions to my dance studies – due to the war – I was never able to continue with my notation studies.

I often regretted this because, as a dancer, teacher and choreographer, I realised more and more that my tutor was absolutely right about the benefits of dance notation in professional life. As time passed I learnt that to notate dancing doesn't mean only to record it – on its own a precious asset to our art form – but much more as well. As a notator cannot record movements without analysing and resolving them into simple elements, notating becomes a valuable aid in the process of learning to dance – in self-correcting, teaching, and creating!

Since this first experience with dance notation many years passed until, after settling in England, I was asked by a friend who was a dancer if she might notate a character-dance choreography I had prepared at the request of the Imperial Society of Teachers of Dancing. I gladly agreed and, as she was one of my demonstrators when I introduced this dance to the ISTD, I was convinced that she would make an excellent job of it on her own. However, to my surprise, day after day she kept asking me for tiny details about certain rhythms, dynamics or movements in my choreography – things of which I was hardly aware!

At first I thought her to be a 'fuss pot', over-anxious about her exam, but later I realised that it was myself who was a bit vague about many of the finer details of the dance. As I repeatedly demonstrated the movements I didn't always execute them exactly in the same manner but, as dancers often do when performing something they know very well, I must have been relying partly on 'routine' and partly on 'instinct'. When it came to analysing the movements it wasn't enough to know sub-consciously how the body should feel when performing the movement; with some more sophisticated refinements I often ended up in a muddle. We needed many hours to sort things out properly.

All this hard labour was far from wasted time and effort. After being obliged to analyse my choreography in such detail I began to find ways of giving more exact explanations and corrections to my students instead of just demonstrating without giving much thought to the actual processes. Now my pupils learnt steps and general technique much more quickly than before and I could make them understand much better the refinements in style, musicality, characterisation and quality. All in all, this episode taught me that analysing movements properly made me a better teacher and it evidently made better dancers of my pupils, student-teachers and their pupils.

Later on I was asked to teach ballet classes once a week in the Institute of Benesh Notation. Though the students' technical standards and their knowledge of classical dancing were rather uneven, my duty was to give them advanced and complicated classes in order to challenge their movement memory and their skills in notation. Our usual practice was that once a week I taught a class in which the students were not allowed to make any notes, and for the following week they had to produce a written record of what they could recall from the previous lesson. They would read, and then demonstrate, all the exercises under my supervision and together we corrected whatever was wrong in their notes while repeating the entire class.

At the beginning, as one would expect, the pupils failed to notate quite a few details, and mixed up the order of exercises, or they inadequately analysed some details of a movement. Surprisingly, in time, they improved in all aspects. In learning some of the most complicated steps through analysis, rather than just trying to copy them, even those less advanced students with bodies which, from a professional point of view, were quite unsuitable, made considerable progress, even in technical execution.

It occurred to me that if these young choreologists, lacking in sufficient technical preparation and suitable physiques, could understand, memorise and make their muscles work in the right order to manage the required steps (although the execution might not be up to the highest standards) then all those talented vocational school students with well-prepared and suitable bodies would make even better progress if they had the benefit of the analytical approach given by dance notation.

Later, the Institute of Choreology asked for my permission to notate my entire character-dance teaching system for their library. I started to work with a young choreologist more or less using the same method adopted with the students. I expected good and fast results but the outcome amazed me beyond belief. Nobody before learnt from me so rapidly the various character exercises and the different styles, and with such precision, quality and style.

Shamefully and regretfully I confess that I am still an 'illiterate' but through these experiences at least I began to understand more and more the wisdom of my teacher's words – that dance notation is the scientific backbone of our art. I became completely convinced that if everyone in our profession – and especially the new generation of teachers – could write and read the same specific notation it would mean we would all become 'literate' in our province: we could record past and present creations, teach systems and classes for future generations, and dancers would be obliged to use their mental capacity more fully while learning the physical skills of their art. This would help them in self-correction and in becoming independent at an earlier age. Also, a future generation of teachers would be able to analyse, and therefore correct more accurately.

If a universally accepted notation became generally adapted in our profession – just as it already is in the musical profession – and if every dance student learnt it simultaneously with their technical studies – as musicians do – dancers, and through them dancing as an art form, could progress in the right direction.

A 'bought' self-confidence

Besides accurate dance-notation systems the twentieth century has brought us other blessings through advanced technology which has enabled us to record and analyse dancing visually by means of film, and in later years by video.

Nowadays dance companies and most vocational schools can afford to own at least one video camera and recorder so, besides recording some repertoire or classes, either for learning purposes or for later reference, the video tapes can be used by dancers to observe the accomplishments of many of their colleagues and they sometimes have a chance to monitor themselves in action. All of this gives them tremendous opportunity to broaden their horizons, to learn more repertoire, old and new, and to watch and compare various productions, different choreographic styles, and differing teaching systems and methods. They can become more critical of their own and other dancers' standards and correct their short-comings. However, one set of equipment can't do it all.

An ideal solution – and it shouldn't be just an Utopian dream for the future – would be if video cameras could be used regularly in all classrooms at vocational schools and at each company rehearsal and performance. The idea makes me jump for joy!

Let us imagine what brilliant prospects our art form would have if we could afford to install one or more video cameras in every classroom and in each auditorium to record and weigh our dancers' achievements, their progress as well as stagnation, success as well as failure. What is more, the dancers could watch it all for themselves, afterwards.

Many teachers may have some doubts about how quickly – if at all – this could be achieved in the impoverished dance world – video equipment is expensive. We can but hope that a more pros-perous future will reduce the price of these machines so that these worthy ideals may be accomplished. In the meantime we should try to find ways by which we can make the best use of what is already available.

When I was making my second video, 'Faults, Corrections, Perfections', I had to work to a ridiculously low budget. Knowing that the most costly part of the procedure was the final editing of the tape, I sat in front of my TV screen, day and night, using the 'slow-motion' and 'freeze-frame' facilities on the equipment to prepare a rough version before the off- and on-line editing began. As I laboured, replaying sections over and over again, viewing shots made about some identical movements, I experienced some-thing incredible – something akin to a scientist investigating a familiar subject under his microscope and realising how little he really knows about it. I could hardly contain my excitement and surprise as I kept on seeing, discovering and learning from the camera's revealing eye. There in front of me was the almost perfect analysis of every movement danced on those tapes. I could study every detail of each movement at various speeds, stopping at any time and for as long as I required. I could make use of the 'close-ups' for easier analysis, repeat things as often as I wished and investigate in the smallest detail the cause of a precise or faulty movement execution. I realised what a wonderful and powerful teaching aid lay in the use of the video camera and recorder and how much easier it was to make the right diagnosis of many faults and find the right remedy for their corrections.

Even if a school or company owns only one piece of equipment there are many ways to make valuable use of this high technology and a few well-chosen tapes which could be of interest for a given age-group of dancers to watch and analyse under the guidance of their teacher. Regularly held tutorials, or perhaps some special 'video classes' could be added to the general timetable. None of this would cost much, it could be easily achieved; it would not put any extra physical stress on the dancers and would be as new and informative for the teachers as for the pupils. The results may prove quite astonishing, however we can gain something of even greater value from this technology.

I was preparing a most promising ballerina and her partner for the leading roles in *Swan Lake*. In spite of her talent and intellect (or because of them) and all my reassurances, she constantly doubted herself – she has always been her own most severe critic. As with so many dancers, her self-confidence was wounded cruelly in the past and it has remained a constant struggle to reinstate it.

At one of the rehearsals she proudly placed a video camera on top of the piano in the corner of the studio, saying, 'I spent all my savings on this 'little thing', but I hope it will help me a lot, not only by stretching my memory but by showing me clearly all my faults.'

'It might even show you some of your assets, or is this camera specially 'programmed' to record only your negative aspects?'

'Well, perhaps not entirely, anyway would you allow us to record all our rehearsals with you from now on? We would like to make sure that we don't forget any of your corrections and suggestions.'

As we worked so did the small object, humbly and quietly, almost forgotten on top of the old piano. A few days later at the next rehearsal I noticed a remarkable improvement – both dancers remembered the vast majority of my criticisms and corrected those faults – and I sensed a quite unusual optimism and self-confidence in the atmosphere.

'Is it possible, after all, that this camera of yours is capable of recording some of your accomplishments as well?'

'I have to admit that it does!' she laughed. 'I couldn't believe my eyes when I watched the tape the other day! It was magic. I witnessed how, in a matter of a few hours, I was transformed from an 'ugly duck' into a quite credible swan.'

'Much more than just 'credible' but into a rather beautiful and moving one,' said her always encouraging partner, 'but you never believe us telling you that you are such a capable dancer until you can see it for yourself through the lens of this camera.'

'Oh, but I did trust your opinion a lot. It's just that I sometimes felt that perhaps you might be biased and may have said so out of kindness to help me out of my desperation.'

'I never thought that money could buy such things as self-confidence,' said I, 'but undoubtedly you've just done it by purchasing this camera. Never was money better spent!'

Most young dancers suffer from a lack of self-confidence even if their teachers try their best assuring them of their talent. In monitoring their progress, by video-recording and then showing them the results, their self- esteem could be greatly enhanced, as well as their performance and maturation.

As human invention produced and developed an alphabet and, much later, music notation, literature and music rapidly progressed over the centuries, masterpieces were created and saved for posterity. The development of printing and writing processes, radio and sound-recording technology, made the accessibility, popularity and advancement of these art forms infinite.

There is now every hope for the art of dance to achieve similar progress, accessibility and therefore wide popularity, if the profession generally would use an universally accepted dance notation together with film and video techniques.

PART 5

PRECONCEPTIONS

———————— ❖ ————————

Pigeonholes

The danger of categorising dancers

A young dancer, job-hunting unsuccessfully after graduation, came to my private studio. She was small and slightly over-weight (mainly 'puppy-fat' due to her late puberty) but her extensions were beautifully placed, she was strong on her *pointes*, had fast, reliable, well-polished *pirouettes*, and her musicality matched her expressive style, quality and intelligence. It was obvious that she was talented, except for one thing – her elevation was almost non-existent. This was surprising as she had well-controlled and quite deep *pliés* and *fondus*.

'It seems there is nothing anyone can do about my jumps,' she said with sad submission. 'All my teachers have given up hope, in spite of the fact that my Achilles tendon is of a normal length. For years I was told that I am, and always will be, one of those *terre-à-terre* type of dancers.' With a typical self-deprecating giggle, known so well in the profession, she added, 'I guess I'll never be a Myrtha. . .'

'Perhaps you are not quite right for that particular role, but I don't see why we shouldn't find a way for you to become a little more airborne.'

I longed to discuss this girl's case with her former teacher – whose work and opinion I valued highly – but this had to wait as she was guest-teaching abroad.

I started by observing in great detail some specific aspects of the girl's technique – breathing, timing, balance-line, weight distribution in the air – areas where some hidden faults might be hindering her *ballon*. Certainly, I found a few. By themselves none could be identified as 'the cause' but, after she had made all the relevant corrections, her *allegro* improved. Though the progress was slight it was enough to give her sorely needed hope, but I knew that I hadn't yet 'hit the nail on the head'.

I was so busy observing and analysing her work during daily practice that it was several weeks before I accidentally discovered what she did immediately before classes and in between exercises.

In her personal 'warm-up' she did innumerable *battements tendus* at such a speed that instead of warming up her ankle, toes, under the instep and the ball of her foot, she just kept moving her leg very fast with the foot in a more or less rigid position. I suggested she should do the exercise at a slower speed and more thoroughly.

Between exercises – though discreetly, almost secretly – she kept shaking and massaging her feet.

'I keep having this slight cramp in my feet from ever since I can remember,' she answered to my query. 'It is terribly irritating, but I was told that as I have strong and healthy feet there is no need to fuss about it, just relax and massage them when it is needed. This way I can keep dancing all day long. You really mustn't worry about it.' But, of course, I did!

I was sure that to ignore a constantly recurring cramp was a big mistake. It also crossed my mind that there might be some connection between the cramp in her feet and the speedy 'warm-up' *tendus* with her inability to jump. I advised her that for a while – but with the exception of special *pointe* and repertoire classes – she should stop wearing *pointe* shoes. Instead she should do her daily *barre* exercises in socks, centre practice in soft shoes, and some of the *petit* and *grand allegro* barefooted.

At first she was a bit reluctant because she had been told one should always wear *pointe*-shoes in class to strengthen the feet, however – after practising for a while in this manner – she admitted that not only had the cramps become less persistent but her jumps required less effort.

By now, a few facts had emerged. Stopping her from exercising numerous, very fast *tendus* before class without being properly 'warmed-up' and in stiff shoes, prevented her feet from becoming rigid and prone to cramp. Working in socks, soft practice shoes or barefooted enabled the girl to use her toes, the neglected and weakened arches, and the balls of her feet. All these changes reduced the cramps within a very short time and helped to improve her elevation and, most importantly, they gave her encouragement and myself reassurance that we might be on the right track.

Next, I examined her *pointe*-shoes and persuaded her to try out a broader fitting with a slightly softer back. A few weeks later the cramp had gone and she had gained a light, springy quality to her jumps, first in the smaller then in the bigger ones.

It was evident that all she needed from now on were some additional exercises to strengthen those parts of her feet which had been neglected, and to make them more pliable. Each day her elevation improved because she was able to inject more power into her feet when taking off and landing.

I could hardly wait to tell her previous teacher the good news and telephoned her at the first opportunity after her return from abroad. I had hardly started the conversation by reminding her of the girl's past difficulty in elevation when she cut in, saying with great sympathy: 'It's a shame that this quite talented girl is so earthbound. All the staff felt sorry for her but we agreed that perhaps she might make it as a *corps-de-ballet* girl in a small company but, unfortunately, she is *one of those* charming 'little dumplings' who will *never ever* be able to get off the ground!'

Oh dear! 'one of those' and 'never ever'. . . I felt too embarrassed to tell my far more experienced senior colleague that this 'earth-bound little dumpling' was by now happily leaping around and showing all the signs of becoming an 'air-borne little gazelle'. I was absolutely sure that there was no cynicism or unkindness behind this teacher's opinion but I considered it fortunate that by mere chance I had been unable to discuss this dancer's situation with her before. If I had had that opportunity, her opinion might have had a negative influence upon my interest and curiosity in finding the key to this dancer's problem as I rated her work and opinions very highly.

Probably I too would have sadly reconciled myself with the thought that this student had little chance of progression. Perhaps I wouldn't have gone to the trouble of finding out what this 'dumpling' was doing for her 'warm-up' before class and in-between exercises. Even if I had noticed some of the symptoms (cramp, lack of power in her feet, etc.) I might have considered these as just additional items in the list of her physical shortcomings instead of trying to connect them together and recognise in them indications for where a solution may lie.

I wondered why this devoted teacher had such a biased attitude? Perhaps she was influenced by this student being a bit plump, or maybe she had been persuaded by some of her practical colleagues that the girl's chances were almost nil; therefore she had placed her in an appropriate pigeonhole and abandoned the search for a solution to the girl's particular problems.

Sadly, this is never just a loss for the student. By failing to seek faults and their remedies for any particular dancer's problem, teachers themselves cease to learn and progress. Having missed the search and cure, the only solution left would seem to be to put even more candidates in pigeonholes!

As it happened, this dancer was lucky: she progressed rapidly, worked correctly and lost her excess weight. She soon found a job in which she was content, and eventually became a soloist.

The Right Criteria for Casting

Preconceived ideas

As we proceed through the various phases of our professional life numerous, differing experiences make us realise how prone we are to 'pigeonhole' students, dancers, teachers and even choreographers by judging them and acting on the basis of preconceived ideas. Such a practice must be harmful, not only to the many individual artists in question but to the progress of Dance generally.

Some time ago after a matinée performance of *Swan Lake* I bumped into one of the most distinguished, elderly teachers of the profession. We exchanged opinions about the interpretations given by the two young artists who had just danced the leading roles for the first time.

'It's an excellent policy of the direction to try out the youngsters at matinée performances,' she said. 'This girl is very capable and technically ready to take on any leading role but, of course, she will never ever be right for this one. . . she'll grow into a lovely soubrette ballerina but she'll never be an Odette/Odile or, for that matter, a leading classical dancer.'

'To give a more mature and refined interpretation she certainly needs a lot of further work and coaching for the role but, considering her youth, I thought that she was quite promising. Sensitivity, lyricism and vulnerability as well as dramatic expression are amongst her qualities.'

'She is no doubt an artist, ideal for such roles as Swanilda, Pineapple Poll, Lise and the like, that was obvious ever since she was a student, but. . . she never has had, nor will have, 'that classical look'. . .'

'I don't quite understand your meaning, The lines of her movements are impeccable, her style is pure, her body is slim and well proportioned, she has highly arched feet and she has a radiantly beautiful face.'

'Yes, yes. But that fair complexion, those blue eyes, blonde hair. . . No, no. Mark my word: I shall be very surprised if she will ever be cast again in this role or any other classical ones – not under this management. . .'

I couldn't believe my ears but I soon realised that there was not much point reasoning with her. Her conviction was fossilised, based neither on the promising performance she had just witnessed nor on the belief that talent and extended study might transform a young dancer's stage image, but rather on some generalised and preconceived ideas. It became obvious, from her unconvincing, almost childish argument, that her views (or misinterpretations) might not even be her own but ones handed down to her, from past teachers whose dated principles were respected unquestionably by herself and many others in the profession.

One would like to think that this incident was just an odd, isolated case – one person's shortsighted view, a harmless comment which didn't count at all in the long run. Indeed it was an extreme example of how a well-meaning and eminent teacher blindly followed some prejudiced ideas. Unfortunately, it was neither isolated nor completely harmless.

As a dancer I have experienced similar situations. As a teacher I have witnessed many such cases and heard of countless different stories of this kind from all over the world, told by many frustrated dancers.

While watching a stage rehearsal of the second act of *The Sleeping Beauty*, I found I was sitting next to one of the older members of the company who had been giving an absolutely outstanding portrayal of Carabosse; he was well known in the profession for his superb interpretations of other grotesque or comical character and mime roles in that company's repertoire. During the interval I congratulated him on his excellent characterisation and we began to chat about the roles which he would prepare for the rest of the season.

'Did you see the cast list for the new Swan Lake?,' he asked. I detected a bitter tone in his voice. 'I'm to be the tutor, yet again.'

'But that is a charming role. . . or have you become a bit tired of it? I'm sure you'll add some fresh colour and flavour.'

'Oh, I've had a lot of fun doing it before and I'll enjoy playing it until I give up dancing. The point is that I always wanted to dance Rothbart, a most intricate character, and this time I had hoped to be given the chance before it is too late for me to cope with the physical side of the role.'

'There is nothing to worry about as far as your technique and stamina are concerned, you are still in perfect condition to do everything that is required of that part. Have you asked for it?'

'As a matter of fact I did but I was told "Never ever!". It's out of the question – Rothbart must be tall – which I am not!'

'Yes, Rothbart is done everywhere by tall men and you are just of average height.' As soon as I had said this I felt there was something quite wrong with my statement. It sounded shallow – a parrot-like phrase. I was repeating a preconceived idea which I believed to be right without giving any consideration to that given situation.

I felt so stupid and ashamed when I heard him saying, 'Funny, I'd have thought that to transform oneself into a sinister, revengeful and magical despot, half-bird and half-man, would need a good interpretative artist and a dominant stage personality rather than a giant. This idea that Rothbart should be tall seems to be inconsistent and a patronising attitude towards the audience. To rate the public so primitive that they identify power, tyranny and viciousness with a tall individual is a bit condescending, isn't it? Besides the whole idea is illogical: in the lakeside scenes Rothbart is supposed to be an owl, but even the largest of owls is nothing like the bigger birds of prey, and they are definitely smaller than swans! To be consistent, Rothbart should not be an owl but an eagle – or some similarly large bird – if they want him to be taller than all the swans. . .'

Suddenly I saw that I had been trying to defend an utterly narrow-minded viewpoint – his assertions were highly intelligent and absolutely valid. It was a great pity that the public were to be deprived of a possibly great, and certainly unconventional, portrayal of Rothbart, and that this exceptional artist should be made unhappy in being prevented from fulfilling a life-long artistic desire. The short figure of Napoleon didn't stop him from becoming the Emperor who brought most of Europe to its knees; neither was Hitler a tall man and he embodied the most cruel tyrant of modern history. Rothbart's characterisation should depend on the talent, intelligence and theatrical skill of the interpreting player (three qualities of which this artist had plenty) as well as on good production – not on a number of feet and inches.

It seems that judging and casting artists on the basis of preconceived and prejudiced thoughts which have put them into 'everlasting' pigeonholes is quite a common practice. If this were not true would one hear so repeatedly such cynical clichés from tired,

impatient or angry répétiteurs, directors or choreographers: 'Why
is it that dancers are so stupid that they never know what type of
roles they are really suited for?' 'Why, oh why, do they always
want to dance something different from the role for which they are
cast?' 'Instead of wasting precious time and energy with constant
moaning and fighting for parts they think they can accomplish,
why can't they be happy enough with what they are given, and get
on with it?'

On the other hand, when listening to soloists and leading
dancers one is painfully aware that their lamentations are often
justified: 'If they'd let me learn this role I'd prove that I can give a
good interpretation! I feel the part in my bones. . .' 'Ever since I
was a student I was considered as a 'classical' type, as a result I
was always cast in the 'classical', serene roles. I like dancing them
but I long to create completely different roles. I feel I could
contribute also to the more dramatic roles and some modern
creations, however, the management don't even consider giving me
such challenges. At least, why don't they let me try?' 'I might give
this role a different characterisation because I am different from
the type of dancer they usually cast for it, but why should that be
inartistic? Why can't I show the role in a different light? After all
we are not dancing to please the management, or the critics, but
for our own artistic fulfilment and to give pleasure and artistic
experience to the audience. Why don't they let the audience judge
for themselves?'

These are not the outcries of silly, immature, impatient,
tiresome and over-ambitious people, they are, more often than not,
justified thoughts, the kind of desires which every serious, self-
respecting, interpretative artist feels. Admittedly, not all dancers'
desires can be justified but giving them some consideration could
be worthwhile. The numerous, mistaken decisions taken by short-
sighted type-casting during an artist's career are mostly irreversible
– due to a dancer's short professional lifespan – and affects the
development of our art form. The loss is mutual. . .

The higher the better ???

A former Soviet ballerina, who was a leading dancer with the
company where I was a guest teacher, asked me to work with her
on the roles of Odette/Odile. In the past, as was usual in Soviet
companies, she had been coached in all her parts by her usual

ballerina-coach but she first performed *Swan Lake* only after leaving Russia, and she never felt secure in the leading role.

'I have danced the Swan Queen a few times but, instead of becoming more relaxed and better at each performance, I am becoming more nervous and insecure. During a performance – while I'm desperately trying to concentrate – my mind pictures a horrible caricature of myself: a freak trying to dance with heavy, earthbound movements. My dancing is ruined. It seems as though two voices are arguing inside me. One says: "Do it," while the other mocks me, "You mustn't, because you look *grotesque!*" Please help! In a few weeks I have to dance the role in our new production and though I'm really longing to perform it, at the same time, I'm petrified.'

I was stunned! A ballerina's whole life revolves around performing movements which should be always harmonious, balanced and beautiful. In this double role the two women – though utterly different in character – should be portrayed as being beautiful, feminine, and irresistible. It is hard to imagine how any sensitive dancer could become both Odette – the idolised embodiment of vulnerable femininity and perfection – as well as Odile – the dazzlingly seductive, purposeful and self-confident beauty – while secretly visualising herself as a grotesque image. How can she possibly convey the majestic movements of a swan either in flight or gliding gracefully on the smooth surface of the lake when some cruel force deep inside makes her feel heavy and earthbound? It must have been sheer hell to be compelled to dance *Swan Lake* while in such an extraordinary state of mind. Her sub-conscious thoughts produced a destructive and paralysing contradiction which resulted in a complete loss of confidence. . . but why?

I sensed that no matter how much we rehearsed, or how much she trusted my opinion, I would never succeed in restoring her self-confidence as far as this ballet was concerned unless I could find out the reason for its loss.

How could such a brilliant artist, respected throughout the profession and admired by international audiences and critics, lose her self-assurance to such a degree, even though she was head-strong and resolute?

She wasn't really worried more than any other responsible ballerina would be about the virtuosity needed in Act III. The quality, style and musicality required for the 'white' acts didn't trouble her too much either – she knew she had all of these gifts. Nor did she fear the dramatic demands of these roles, she was a natural actress and enjoyed acting. As for stamina, she had plenty of experience in preparing her strength for demanding ballets such as this. What was she afraid of? Heavy!. . . Earthbound!. . . Grotesque!. . . Freak!. . . what could be the reason for her to associate these idioms with herself and why only in this ballet?

'Perhaps you felt unsafe because you were faced with a very demanding role without the benefit of guidance from your usual coach in Soviet Russia, whom you trusted, and who knew your assets as well as shortcomings?' I asked.

'Not really! Our relationship wasn't exactly ideal. She might have crushed rather than built up my confidence!'

'Oh?' Is this a lead, I wondered?

'Anyway, since I came to the West I learnt and danced several parts which had not been in my repertoire. I've worked with a number of different choreographers and coaches and so far it has turned out quite well with all my new roles. . . except *Swan Lake*!'

'Can you describe exactly what images come to your mind when you feel earthbound and grotesque on stage?'

'Each time I do all those millions of *arabesques, attitudes* and *penchés* I see myself doing them even lower than usual and with a distorted body-line. These images disturb me so much that I can't concentrate on artistic matters. While doing the movement sequences automatically all I can think of is how some of the professionals sitting in the audience must pity me, how they will compare my horrible, low and ugly *attitudes* and *arabesques* to those of other dancers, how futile my efforts are, what a mistake it was for me to accept this role, and. . .'

'You are probably suffering from that fashionable and contagious illness which is sweeping through the world of dance and which we may call 'extensionitis', the belief that the higher the legs go the better the dancer is! I admit that your extensions are not your forte but they are not as low as you are trying to make them out to be and, more to the point, they are beautifully placed and create perfect classical lines.

'There were famous ballerinas, like Ulanova and Fonteyn, who were great interpreters of Odette/Odile and had similar, perhaps even lower, extensions in these positions than you have at the moment, and it didn't matter at all. They had much more to offer their audiences than high 'attibesques'. They were extraordinary artists who were able to compensate for this one shortcoming a hundred times over. It may be very impressive for a ballerina to have high extensions but, surely, the height of *arabesques* and *attitudes* should not be the criteria of an artistic portrayal of this role.

'The general image of a swan is best portrayed by imitating the gliding effect on the water (*bourrée*ing), the movements of the wings in flight (*ports de bras*), and the typical bird-like neck and head movements. None of these requires hyper extensions of the legs, do they? I believe that the advice of the French composer Rameau to his musicians and singers, "Don't impress, but touch me," is a wise one and should be followed by every interpretative artist.'

She looked at me. 'I wouldn't quarrel for a moment with these artistic principles and logic. I could wish that audiences and professionals would agree with us since, nowadays, it is mostly taken for granted that a ballerina who dances *Swan Lake* must have super-high extensions! My teachers, including my coach who excelled in these roles, told me never ever even dream of dancing them because of my limited *arabesques* and *attitudes*.' She added with a touch of sadness, 'Indeed, when compared with the capabilities of my colleagues and my coach, I felt I looked like Quasimodo and reconciled myself to the fact that I would never ever become a Swan Queen.'

'But since then several companies have asked you to dance this part as their guest ballerina, in spite of your relatively low 'attibesques'. They wouldn't have asked you if they didn't think you would be a great success as Odette/Odile. This should have given you enough confidence.'

'It did to a certain point, and that's why I agreed, after some hesitation, to dance it. During the initial rehearsals I had hopes and doubts – as one does with every new role – but I didn't have this grotesque, disabling vision of myself. It hits me only when it really matters, at performances. . .'

'Perhaps, unknown to yourself, you feel 'guilty' because you dare to dance a role which your mentors consider not suitable for you. To punish you for dancing it your sub-conscious mind creates this Quasimodo-like image just when you are actually committing the 'crime' – performing the 'forbidden ballet'!'

By now she was overcome with emotion. Her voice failed. Fighting her tears she could only nod her head to let me know that we had found the root of her problems.

Now I could begin to devise a 'strategy' which might help her fight the reappearance of Quasimodo.

To uncover the source of dancers' psychological problems and then make them recognise it, is for both teacher and artists not only revealing but a comprehension of their common enemy and hence a recognition of 'whom', 'what' and 'how' to fight. For the dancer it helps to combat consciously the disabling creations of their sub-conscious and then to face the reality with a positive attitude. For the coach it serves as a compass, showing where to direct the artist's concentration in order to find the way to victory.

I realised that in the specific case of this seriously troubled ballerina I had to devise a special kind of 'coaching technique'. I had to find a modus operandi which would help me prepare her for the roles of Odette/Odile in this particular *Swan Lake* and, at the same time, which would also assist the healing of her past mental injuries and restore her self-confidence.

Up to a certain point I needed to understand that her anxiety about raising the height of her *attitudes* and *arabesques* wasn't without some reason. For a ballerina of her calibre some progress in this particular issue would be useful as well, as it would help to diminish her psychological complexes. I was curious to see if it was possible to make her back more pliable, thereby enhancing her extension to a higher degree, so I gave her some special exercises to increase the flexibility of her spine.

We both knew that if she wanted to avoid injuries these efforts would come to fruition (if at all) only in a slow and gradual manner, but there were only a few weeks before her performances, therefore I had to plan my second move most carefully. I was convinced that it was paramount to reassure her that there were other, far more pre-eminent issues to which she should devote her talent, energy, time and concentration than the dreaded *attitudes* and *arabesques*.

I called her attention to the physical and psychological elements in the roles – areas where her special qualities could easily equal, and even improve on in certain aspects, the portrayals of those excellent ballerinas whose brilliant interpretations she admired and respected.

My criticism and corrections were always honest but I took every opportunity to build up her shattered self-confidence by emphasising that besides her strong stage personality she possessed plenty of other gifts, all to her advantage: her physical beauty (looking very delicate and as light as a feather); her long neck which she used with immense grace; her long arms and legs, even though she was small in stature; her virtuosity (her thirty-two *fouettés* were devilishly fast while she alternated the single turns with doubles); her *pirouettes* of all kinds were full of bravura; her balances were beautifully held for as long as necessary.

We spent a considerable time just talking about the roles in general, discussing how she saw the two contrasting personalities and how she could fit her own ideas into the forthcoming production.

We agreed that the basic characteristics for both Odette and Odile can be found more or less in all of us as they are the traits of 'the eternal woman'. In order to give a true and original inter-pretation of these two women one needs only to search one's inner self to find the core of their typical features, bring them to the surface, and magnify or minimise them with theatrical skill, according to which character one is portraying.

We finally concluded that if a ballerina's main goal was to interpret truthfully these two separate personalities by dancing in style and using the choreographic imagery bring across the deep message of the drama, then the height of an *attitude* or *arabesque* cannot become a crucial issue!

Knowing that dancers normally give priority to working on the physical aspects of their role to build up their strength and stamina, I was glad to see that she didn't think it a waste of precious time just talking in such detail about interpretation of the role at our first few rehearsals.

Discussing these matters also helped us to get to know one another as human beings. In turn this created an intimate working-relationship which helped to relax her mind and inspired her creativity. Soon I noticed that she produced some individual images of a rare quality – something which often happens with talented interpreters under favourable circumstances. I brought this to her attention and, by memorising and adding these details to her interpretation, her portrayal gained an individual and unique flavour.

As her confidence grew she began to consolidate her character-isations by consciously incorporating all sorts of slight changes, in *ports de bras*, accenting movements, and the direction and length of a glance when relating to Siegfried or Rothbart.

Soon her mentions of 'ugly and low extensions' were supplanted by her interest in how she could make 'herself fit the role' and 'the role fit her' by using her individual talent and technique.

We made the best use of her long neck and arms by connect-ing the specific 'swan' *port de bras* with the correct breathing in order to give her dancing a greater flow and her flying and gliding movements more ethereal. We analysed how different uses of the neck and head can not only imitate bird-like movements but also how it can help to express both Odette's suffering, fears, surprise, vulnerability, love, even her dignified royal behaviour, as well as Odile's scheming, cunning, mocking and triumphant sensuality.

To convey the emotions, moods, thoughts and action of the two different characters in a way that suited her physique and personality we drew on her strong technique and musicality. Instead of being 'ashamed' of the low line of her *arabesques* she used her beautifully controlled balances with them, while following with her arms and upper body movements the musical melody, or certain accents and rhythms, even the different sounds of certain leading instruments in the score's orchestration.

From that point on I was confident that I was witnessing the beginning of an exceptionally moving and beautiful interpretation of a vulnerable Odette and a uniquely witty, calculating and dazzling Odile, but I wasn't quite so sure yet whether she had fully recovered from her serious mental injuries. In rehearsals she was very positive and seemed to be on the mend but we both knew that the real test would be at the first performance – will Quasimodo return or not?

After the general rehearsal she said with an 'impish' expression, 'I wish I could dance *Swan Lake* now with my old teachers and coach watching!'

It was clear from these words that the poisonous 'never ever' had ceased to have any effect on her, that her self-confidence was restored and she wasn't suffering any more from 'extensionitis', nor was the vision of that grotesque freak likely to disturb her lovely portrayal of Odette/Odile – a role which audience, critics and professional colleagues agreed was sensational and perhaps her best interpretation of a role so far in her career.

'Never ever' is an expression which a teacher should *never ever* use. It is a negative statement which can cause serious, and long-lasting, mental injuries affecting a dancers' artistic output. Also one must guide with prudence and vision the artistic taste of students and dancers – which subsequently will influence the opinions of both audiences and critics – as far as high extensions are concerned.

PART 6

THE TRIANGLE

———————— ❖ ————————

Vivaldi's Choice

Co-operation between parents, teacher and student

Little is known about the life of the Venetian composer Antonio Vivaldi, so I have often wondered what his reasons were for spending the greater part of his enormously creative life in teaching music at a home for girls born out of wedlock. Why did he compose an endless repertoire of masterpieces for the orchestra of this orphanage, which – since the school's inhabitants were chosen for their personal situation rather than for their musical ability – must have been rather limited in real talent?

Did Vivaldi compromise because he was unaware of his outstanding artistic values? As his sometime collaborator, the dramatist Carlo Goldoni, described in his memoirs that he had a 'childishly vain' character, that is most unlikely.

To solve this contradiction I let my imagination run wild and tried to find some rational reasons. Perhaps this infamous vanity was a façade to hide self-doubt and insecurity and he was so much afraid of failure of any kind that he would rather not work with professional musicians. Maybe a wish for a simple, sheltered life and a secure means of subsistence was stronger than any ambition for fame, or was he afraid of the temptations to be found in the notoriously frivolous Venetian way of life? Could there have been a secret romance going on behind the walls of the institution? Was one of the girls his daughter? The list grew even longer until, by chance, it seemed that I discovered a possible and practical solution. . .

I was still actively dancing but I wanted to spread my wings a bit as a teacher by regularly giving a few classes at a well-established ballet school. After some time one of the most talented students began to fall behind in her work. Something was seriously disturbing this sincere and diligent girl; she began to lack physical energy, her concentration often wandered, and she became moody, untidy in looks and clothing, unobservant (either staring with a vacant expression or near to tears), and often late arriving for class. Being inexperienced as a teacher, I sought the advice of my colleagues.

'She's probably reaching a difficult stage of puberty. You should scold her for being so undisciplined and don't fuss or pamper her, otherwise the rest of the class will follow suit, wishing for more attention. Just ignore her!'

But I couldn't. I had a feeling that there was more to this girl's situation than the usual unpleasant symptoms of puberty. Several times I tried to talk with her but that usually resulted in bucketfuls of tears. Finally I resolved to speak with her mother.

For several days I had no response to my request for a meeting. Determined to find out the cause for this girl's distressed state I decided to visit her home. There I found several bewildered children in the company of their drunken father. Shocked, I managed to glean from the barely intelligible and fragmented conversation some sad facts. The children's pregnant mother had been in hospital for some time, being treated for a particularly nasty beating from her violent husband, and they were being looked after by their eldest stepsister – my student.

Some days later the poor woman contacted me directly, a simple but very intelligent and caring mother. She told me that her second husband was basically a good-hearted man but, when drunk, he resorted to violence and he now refused to give his step-daughter the financial help she needed to continue her dance studies.

Soon we formed a very positive relationship and by our joint efforts, although we couldn't alter their pitiable circumstances, we were able to give to her daughter enough understanding, assurance and love to make this youngster feel more protected and confident for the future. She became her better self again and I encouraged her to apply for a scholarship. Her depression changed to a powerful sense of vocation. She worked extremely hard and matured artistically. Instead of being the disruptive element in the class she became a good example, positively influencing many of her classmates who also might have acquired depression through puberty.

This incident made me realise for the first time that one cannot be satisfied only by teaching students in the artificially detached, almost sterile atmosphere that is often found in a vocational school. In order to form young dancers into real artists one must relate to each of them as a whole human being connected to a life outside the protective walls of the studios, and this can rarely be achieved without having some contact with the pupil's parents. There and then I took a solemn pledge that I would try to follow these principles in the future.

Although it was time-consuming and often depressing, it was usually worthwhile to find out the background of problematic students. Knowing more about them helped me to help them. But, as far as any involvement was concerned, I found out the hard way that one has skilfully to find the right balance.

Parents react in different ways. It is most satisfying when they are positive and recognise that our efforts to build up a relationship are for the benefit of their offspring and when, if they are willing to listen, they collaborate and lend support without taking advantage, or imposing on the teacher's time and energy. However, often this is not the case.

Many parents react negatively. Some feel the teacher is intruding on their private life (discussions may reveal intimate details about family affairs), others' parental pride is dented if one's opinion differs from theirs, and some are simply jealous of their child's respect and love. There are parents who are prejudiced against the dance profession as a whole and snub a dance teacher's ideas, and there are those who are 'too busy' to find precious time for a 'busybody' teacher's over-reactions. . .

To break these barriers, win their confidence and build a good relationship, one needs to educate parents. Not an easy task and one which often proves to be time-consuming.

However, there are types of parent who are more difficult, exhausting, often nerve-wracking than any other. These are the too-anxious, over-supportive or blindly ambitious types, the ones who request special attention and frequent interviews and who believe their children are superior to those of everyone else. They may start all sort of intrigues and disturbances and they will haunt you with their constant lamentations, arguments and aggressive possessiveness.

I remember vividly one particular individual who sorely tried my patience. He pestered me for weeks on end in spite of all my efforts to assure him that his daughter's talent was appreciated by every member of the staff, that she was correctly assessed and received as much attention as any other student – if not more – and that neither her teachers nor her fellow students wished to, or could, hinder her progress. There was no escape, he would wait for me at the entrance to the building, or at the Underground station. I received letters, 'phone calls – at home as well as at the school. I, quite literally, began to hide from him. It was obvious that I had failed to strike the right balance in this particular parent-teacher relationship. After one very exhausting day I was so tired that I forgot my usual precautions. The dreaded parent approached and began to talk. For some time I couldn't concentrate on anything he said, only on my own thought: 'How I wish I could teach dancing in an orphanage! Vivaldi certainly made the right choice.'

Suddenly the man's tiresome voice came to a halt. From his shocked expression I realised that I must have spoken my thoughts out aloud. He must have thought I was out of my mind, I was convinced I had come to my senses!!!

Even today only a few vocational schools recognise the need for more familiarity with their pupils' circumstances and the way these may affect their charges. In these organisations specially trained experts – school counsellors – are engaged to help students and staff to build bridges of understanding between staff and parents, student and teacher, student and parents. These take the form of open days, interviews and counselling sessions.

Unfortunately, in the world of ballet there are still many establishments where there are no counsellors, or their work is too much restricted and isolated from both dance-staff and parents. In many of the better-known company-attached vocational schools – especially where tuition is free – parents are not often allowed any insight into life inside the school. Instead of being involved and educated to know more about this special world and the problems their children will have to face, they are kept away from them as much as possible – the motto being, 'The less we have to deal with parents, the better dancers we can produce!' I recall one annoyed mother asking the director of a world-famous school, 'Is my son going into quarantine for the next seven years, or is it me who has the plague?'

---- ❖ ----

Consequences of Parental Behaviour

And save us from the 'ballet mum'

When I was a student a very quiet and sincere girl joined our class in the middle of the academic year. Although she came from a different school she quickly adapted her work in style and technical matters to our ways, not an easy thing to do in mid term. Before long she was considered by both staff and students to be an 'ideal pupil'. In spite of her rapid advance, none of us felt envious of her talent, physical suitability and beauty because she wore her success so modestly. The one problem the teachers had was with her introvert personality; her shyness was commented upon as a potential disadvantage to her future as an interpretative artist.

We were all at that age when lasting friendships are easily made but, though she seemed a charming, well-meaning girl, none of us became a close friend of hers. We were unaware of the reasons for our own natural reserve and we probably hardly noticed her isolation and just took it for granted that she was by nature withdrawn and friendless. We were also used to seeing her mother around, whereas most other parents stayed away from school except for those occasions when they were expected to be present.

Every day the mother would accompany her daughter to and from school or the theatre and every time there were any displays, demonstrations or concerts, she would be there. It seemed she was everywhere – in all the backstage areas, the canteen, the ticket office, the costume workshops – wherever she had the chance to watch over her daughter's professional activities.

Obviously she was watching out for any possible danger which, in her opinion, might harm her offspring's progress. She was determined to grease the way to future success and, quite shamelessly, she took the opportunity to tell all and sundry, whoever they might be, of her child's superiority.

When I first noticed this behaviour I didn't quite appreciate the

150

comical, almost grotesque, side to it as I secretly envied the girl for having such a 'supportive' mum (my own parents had some misgivings about my choice of career). However, as time passed, it became clear that this woman's behaviour was proving to be an utter nuisance within the whole dance faculty. There were rumours that the staff at the girl's previous school couldn't tolerate the mother's conduct, not even for the sake of her talented child.

Quite often the woman loitered around the staffroom so that she could 'catch' an unsuspecting teacher for a conversation. Nor was it unusual to hear her high-pitched voice asking admittance to the director's office or making arrangements for a future appointment. We weren't surprised to see the irritated expression on the faces of any of the staff when they kept 'bumping' into her unexpectedly.

All of this became very embarrassing for her shy and sensitive daughter. I felt sorry for her and began to understand why this talented young dancer had become such an introvert. (I stopped being envious of her mother's 'support' and counted my blessings that my cool-headed and critical parents had left me alone to get on with my chosen vocation by myself.)

One day, to my surprise, I was invited by the mother to have tea at their home. My first reaction was to find some suitable excuse not to go but I then noticed the daughter's almost pleading expression. It was as if she wanted to say to me something like: 'Please don't mind my mother! I want to be friends, so come for my sake!' Suddenly I understood not only why she was so shy but also that not having friends wasn't her choice, it was her mother's conduct and constant presence which deterred other young people from wishing to have a friendship with the girl.

I agreed to visit them the following weekend.

My school friends were surprised when I told them about my decision and, though many of them sympathised with the poor girl, some of the older and more cynical ones started to tease me, 'You should have your head examined. You are letting yourself be drawn into the web of one of the most dangerous species, the legendary 'Ballet-mum'!'

'You are as good as dead. Nothing'll stop this woman getting rid of one of her daughter's most obvious rivals. She'll try to poison you. Don't touch any of the food and drink she'll offer!'

'Maybe it isn't murder – not just yet – she is cunning. Injuring you 'by chance' might be her tactic. Watch the chair before you sit down, wear rubber soles as the floor might be over-polished. . .' The extreme ideas kept pouring out.

In spite of all this endless mocking, I kept my promise. I spent a whole afternoon at their home – the longest, most boring and frustrating one of all my youth – but I never had an opportunity to have even a single minute alone with my new friend – Mum was always present. Indeed, I don't remember hearing the girl's voice at all until it was time to go, when she said, 'Please, come again soon.' Apart from those few formal words she had no chance at all to say anything. It was pathetic! The mother chose the subjects for our conversation, suggested which dance books we should read – and which we should only browse through – spoke about which of our teachers and classmates were praiseworthy and which deserved avoidance, commented on our schedules, whom we should treat as our dance idols and whom not, and how we should evaluate classical technique and choreography when compared with contemporary work. . .

From time to time she interrupted her 'lecture' to ask me some questions but hardly ever listened to my answers and when I tried to address some questions to her daughter – I wanted to know her opinion on some matters so that I could find out more about her – before the girl could even open her mouth, Mum had already answered them.

At the time I thought her to be the most unbearable sample of her kind. I was too inexperienced in these matters to recognise that this 'monster' was actually one of the mildest and comparatively harmless representatives of the breed! Though she was a pain in the neck, ridiculous, irritating, and often wasted people's time, she was not malevolent. The only person she actually harmed seriously was the one she adored – her own daughter. By being so possessive, bossy, ambitious and over-supportive, she not only turned her child's life into misery but she suppressed her personality, isolated and deprived her of the company of friends and, unforgivably, withheld this young dancer's personal, sexual and artistic maturation.

Dynasties

The concord and collaboration between a teacher and a student's parents affect the achievement of the pupil in every field of education. This correlation is just as important as the mutual understanding between pedagogue and student and it supports the parent/child relationship as well.

If any of these bonds is neglected or missing – or the contrary

happens and they are overdriven – it will cause emotional disturbances in one or more members of this triangular relationship.
Consequently the fine balance needed for tuition and learning
can, at some point or another, tip over. In an unbalanced atmosphere most of the youngsters will fall below the required average
standard. They will find it difficult to gain sufficient self-
confidence to develop a strong personality, or to stretch themselves to achieve an individual best, never mind surpassing it. In
these circumstances their teachers and parents will be obliged to
lower their expectations and valuable potential may remain
hidden until it is too late to bring it to the surface – a vicious circle
is formed.

When an ideal bond is forged between teacher and parent, and
the youngster receives interest, understanding and encouragement
from both sides, the result may be something outstanding. In the
past this has happened repeatedly, specially where the parents had
some vocational occupation and enhanced their children's
education with the same or similar interests. Offspring often
follow in their parents' footsteps in all walks of life from
businessmen to clowns, circus acrobats to doctors, scientists,
teachers, lawyers, preachers, and so on....

This phenomenon frequently occurs in the arts also, though in
the fields of literature and fine arts there are only a few instances.
In the world of opera there are some examples: the Domingos,
Fassbaenders, and the Garcia-Malibran-Viardot family, but there
are more than plenty in the areas of theatre and film – to mention
but a few there are the Chaplins, Redgraves, Minellis and Fondas.

However, it is remarkable that in the art of music and dance we
can find the greatest dynasties spreading over several generations.
The most apparent explanation for this circumstance is that dance
and music are the art forms in which it is paramount that the
acquisition of technical skills should start in childhood.

To substantiate this theory one needs only to remember a few
obvious examples from the vast list of families which have given
humanity such geniuses as the Bachs, Mozarts, Strausses,
Menuhins, Torteliers, Oistrakhs and Kleibers in the musical field.
In the history of dance the Taglionis, Bournonvilles, Petipas,
Nijinskys spring immediately to mind and today – since the art of
dance has spread so widely – we can boast of many dance
dynasties all over the world.

In some of the oldest continental ballet ensembles one finds
that the exceptional talent for dance has spread over three genera-

tions; the inclusion of in-laws and godchildren, and intermarriages between dynasties make these families grow even larger.

If one is involved with the dancing profession, either as a student, parent or teacher, one might look on these families with admiration as well as a certain envy. It seems that the younger generations have inherited the dancing genes of their predecessors and with the influence and encouragement of their parents, grandparents and godparents, their success in the 'family vocation' is assured.

Undoubtedly, the artistically impregnated atmosphere in these homes, as well the constant evidence of the older generation's exemplary dedication, must have played just as important a role in the youngster's progress as their talent-saturated genes. However, it would be a mistake to conclude that in supporting and helping one's child in the study of any art subject – either as an amateur or as a vocational student – the parent has to be a professional artist of the same art form.

The general public is hardly aware that the truth of this matter is often just the opposite. In the majority of cases the talent and fame of celebrated artist-parents and the accompanying 'sensation-chasing' publicity and hero-worship may well act as an intimidating 'depressant' on the unformed personality of their budding offspring.

In some dance dynasties it often happens that a dancer-parent becomes the vocational teacher of their offspring for a certain period of training. At that stage there is a risk that the unwitting parent-teacher's dominant personality suppresses the child-pupil's individual character. This may well cause an inferiority complex which will impede their talent coming to the fore. On the whole, youngsters from these families seem to make much better progress with teachers from outside their own family.

It is also very true that non-artist parents – if they have an interest in the art form their child is studying – can become a tremendous support and a motivating force in the artistic education as well as the character-forming procedure for a young student. Certainly, the overwhelming majority of children studying an art form with enthusiasm, and receiving good results and possible professional success, have parents who are not artists of any kind.

Many famous artists often mention with great reverence and gratitude in interviews and memoirs the tremendous moral support and devotion which they received from their 'ordinary' parents during their student years and even through their professional career. A typical example would be dancer/choreographer Mark Morris and his mother or, for the musicians, conductor Sir Simon Rattle and his father.

These parents are not the unpleasant, pushy, possessive and over-dominant types, nor the grotesque, harmful, over-zealous ones, they simply wish to be involved, and to take part in the interests or the vocational calling of their child. The benefits of such parental support could be most significant. However, parents often shy away from becoming more involved in their children's dance-education because they come up against a certain discouraging attitude. In the past, at company-attached schools all over the world, and also in highly-reputed private establishments, parents were kept as far as possible at bay.

In her autobiography (*Out of Step*, Melbourne University Press, 1993) the Australian ballerina Alida Belair recalls the uncompromising behaviour of Madam Xenia Borovansky at the time of her admittance as a six-year-old to the celebrated teacher's renowned school: 'Madam Borovansky had already made it clear that my development as a dancer was *her* responsibility, and that **she did not tolerate interference from lay people, parents or no**' (my emphasis).

Alas, this kind of attitude hasn't changed much since then!

It is essential that in the future teachers should try to educate and wholly involve parents in learning and recognising the specific problems concerning their child's training. Once they understand the temporary difficulties in connection with the physical, emotional and mental demands placed upon the youngster at a given stage in their studies, they might be able to give them an objective moral support. In the world of dance there is more need for boosting a dancer's self-confidence than in any other art form. To this goal both teacher and parents must work together. If the latter could become more dance-orientated in their interests, with more patience and understanding towards their child's and the teacher's problems – and if at the same time teachers would introduce the parents to the complex issues of a dance-student's education and seek their collaboration more often –the results could, in time, become extraordinary.

Shared experience

I was a member of the Ballet Faculty of the School of Fine Arts in Banff, Canada, for a few consecutive summers in the 1960s.

Although this was only a summer course the minimum age for enrolment at all the faculties was over fifteen years as it was part of the University of Alberta.

During one summer I was astonished by a most unusual sight: every morning the university campus was invaded by numerous infants, aged between three and five, and most of them were carrying half-size violins. There were some young adults present as well – they were carrying violins and violas of a conventional size, together with some sheets of music – and they were ushering the tiny tots towards the Music Building. I wondered what these extraordinarily young 'music candidates', together with the adults, could be up to?

My curiosity was soon satisfied when I was allowed to observe one of their lessons. To my amazement the music teacher wasn't tutoring the infants, only the adults, who turned out to be the children's parents. The youngsters were not told what to do in the class, but if they wanted to join in the grown-ups activities they were encouraged to use their own violins. Afterwards the teacher explained to me that she followed the Suzuki method of violin teaching – which was almost unknown in the West at that time.

A few weeks later I saw something unbelievable: these two generations of 'students' were playing their violins together like a huge string orchestra. The work they performed was by no means technically demanding and it wasn't played with absolute perfection, but the participants were totally, and happily, absorbed in this shared artistic experience. Considering that neither parents nor their children were selected for their special talent for music, and that there were about twenty offspring who were under the age of four, this was a magical result!

With a moment or two of thought, it wasn't too difficult to grasp that behind this 'miracle' there was no 'magic', only common sense. Babies learn to walk, talk and perform many other very complicated and practical activities essential for their survival by observing what their elders do. Children learn fastest and best when their natural curiosity and self-imposed discipline lets them instinctively mimic their parents and siblings without pressure and stress.

Earlier in this century, Mr Suzuki – a distinguished Japanese classical violin player – utilised this fact in an ingenious way. By making the parents study and practise their violin playing regularly in the presence of their children, music-making became a part of family life. The little ones spontaneously mimicked this activity and found it 'good fun'.

What I witnessed nearly forty years ago was the realisation of an ingeniously simple theory; if music-making is a part of everyday life and the motivation to practise stems from both parents' and children's creativity, then youngsters of an unusually young age – even those with just average musicality – are capable of playing one of the most difficult musical instruments in an extraordinarily short period of time. This point is proven best, perhaps, in the life of East European gypsy communities. Music-making, apart from being a source of income, is their natural way of amusement and all infants play musical instruments without being specially taught.

Beginning to learn the basics of any art form (including dancing!) as an infant, through the procedure of mimicking one's parents and siblings, must mean much more to youngsters than either learning some new and practical skills by rote or just having 'fun', though these reasons are essential in everyday life. These studies – by their artistic nature – also awaken in children a multitude of emotions and moods, and help them in self-expression as well as in forming a definite and confident personality at an exceptionally tender age. At the same time the parents become more knowledgeable and appreciative of the chosen art form.

My genuine enthusiasm was spoiled with only a slightly envious thought: why haven't we dance teachers devised some similarly wonderful method?

If we wish dance to survive into the twenty-first century and enjoy a flourishing renaissance, we need to nurture more and better, happy young dancers as well as a wider and far more knowledgeable, critical and demanding audience. What better way to achieve this goal than to involve and educate two generations simultaneously. This method of teaching would also provide the best opportunity for those few youngsters who are blessed with exceptional talents because it would start a very early preparation for their vocation under ideal circumstances.

Since I first encountered the Suzuki method my varied teaching experiences have convinced me that the essence of this astute system could and should be carefully adapted to dance. However, if this should happen, I am aware that the period of experimentation would suffer from more than the usual 'teething problems' which occur when new methods are tried out.

Apart from the customary difficulties – seeking financial backing for a group of competent professionals to prepare the experimental work; convincing those establishments which create the syllabi to allow for certain risks in the introduction of a new method; persuading and re-training teachers to learn and then teach it – it may not be easy to find parents and children willing to volunteer for an experiment which may last for several years. It will be even harder to convince parents who have had no previous training in their younger days to overcome a fear of active involvement in such a specific physical activity as dancing.

It is possible and enjoyable for an adult to learn and play any instrument, or to sing, paint or carve at an amateur level, but most people would be of the opinion that for an adult to learn dancing, even as a beginner, would be difficult, if not impossible, and fairly hazardous from a health point of view. One can understand these scruples if one believes that the highly sophisticated and physically demanding classical ballet technique is the only one to be learnt as a foundation for dance studies. However, this is a very narrow-minded and mistaken theory as there are several more suitable techniques such as natural movement lessons, national and character dancing, historical dance studies, body control and corrective exercises at an elementary level and the Dalcroze System. These are all not only harmless but beneficial and enjoyable ways of dancing, suitable techniques for the body of a young adult as well as an infant. By the time a youngster achieves the age when physique and mind are capable of coping with classical ballet or other sophisticated dance techniques the parents' presence at the dance class is no longer needed and the student can prepare physically, mentally and emotionally for more serious studies.

When children at a delicate age find themselves in harmonious circumstances where there is co-operation, understanding and a shared interest between parents, teacher and themselves as part of an artistic experience, their response to art and creativity is bound to be affected. This method of teaching – involving parents and children simultaneously – could provide a better preparation for nurturing young artists and may create a larger and more appreciative public, people who will love, understand and promote the art of dancing. What a fantastic further prospect this could be for Dance!

PART 7

A REVALUATION OF DANCE AS AN ART

❖

Classical Style – Class, Rehearsal and Performance

Style awareness

I slipped during a performance and fell flat on my face in a most ungraceful position – arms and legs apart in the widest second position imaginable, looking just like a dead frog! With tears streaming down my cheeks I was inconsolable as I came off-stage and bumped into the ballet master. Luckily for me he hadn't witnessed my disgrace. Trying to keep a straight face as he sympathetically listened to my bitter laments, he said, 'My dear girl, if you were spread-eagled on the floor in a *fully turned out* position and if you raised yourself with a pure classical *style* to a clear *épaulement*. . . there is certainly nothing to worry about!' I managed a few giggles through my tears!

I can't help remembering this funny, but typical, incident when I discuss problems concerning the classical ballet style in class, rehearsal or performance.

All over the world classical dancers are trained in several different systems (Cecchetti, Vaganova, Royal Academy of Dancing, Bournonville, Legat, etc.). The corresponding syllabi not only differ greatly from each other in the methods by which they train dancers but there are considerable differences in their styles.

When we assess the revival of an old ballet or an individual interpretation of certain roles in an old production, we seem to take it for granted that we all have the same knowledge, opinion and taste about the particular style in which certain classical choreographies should be interpreted.

Talking about the classical style, we might all agree on a few principal points and we would certainly all condemn such things as mannered or fussy *ports de bras*, lifted shoulders, broken wrists, dropped elbows, untidy positions in footwork, indefinite body directions, a laboured technique, inharmonious head and neck positions or necks that are too stiff, an absence of lightness, and clumsy, obvious partnering. At the same time we would unanimously praise performers who dance with a natural ease and noble elegance using pure classical lines.

There are also a few points where we might disagree. Amazingly, these are not highly sophisticated issues but basic ones: how a high leg-extension may be considered vulgar by some and not others; how much turn-out would be correct in old classical ballets from a stylistic point of view; should *pirouettes* and *chainés* be executed *en pointe* in the works of Bournonville; should *pointe*-shoes be shiny or matte in the classics?

In practice, however, within the world of classical dancing we need to realise that some definitions ('mannered' *port de bras* or 'pure classical' lines for example) may mean *different* things to *different* people. Our taste is formed not only by our individual personality, it is strongly influenced by our upbringing in the various systems. Also, many of these major systems keep changing their syllabi and most of the time these alterations affect both technical matters and style. Consequently, in the interpretation of classical and romantic ballets, our opinions about what the right style is might not only be very different from each other but might also change within a relatively short time.

Dancers trained at the Paris Opéra would have very different ideas about, say, a 'classically pure *attitude* line' from those of dancers trained in the Vaganova system – as far as the placement of the pelvis and the raised leg are concerned. Dancers brought up with the Cecchetti method wouldn't agree with either of the images created by the French or Russian dancers. Cecchetti-trained dancers place the lower part of the body *as well as* the arm, head and shoulder differently to achieve a line they consider to be both correct and beautiful.

These controversial ideas regarding 'pure classical lines' are no less intriguing amongst the dancers of the Bolshoi and Kirov ballet companies. In spite of these dancers studying nothing but the Vaganova syllabus for over seven decades their interpretations of the traditional repertoire are remarkably different with respect to elegance and refinement. For example, Kirov dancers, whose style is the more moderate and refined, may not approve of the uniquely accented wrist-movements and hand-positions of most Bolshoi members. At the same time many of the head and arm positions, which in the past were typical of the style of Vaganova-trained dancers in both companies, have been changed or lost.

The style of dancers brought up within the Bournonville tradition differs a great deal from that manifest in the rest of the classical dancers' world; what's more, Bournonville dancers themselves are in constant disagreement with one another about quite a few stylistic issues.

As well as the pressing time factor in vocational training it would seem to be impossible to study constructively and efficiently all the major classical ballet systems within the format of regular daily classes without causing quite a bit of confusion in the concept of style – the very thing one wishes to keep crystal clear in the student's minds!

The problem of style tends to become more and more stressful. In the past it was sufficient to acquire classical and character dance techniques and styles, and in addition to have some knowledge of the fundamentals of classical mime in order to become a professional dancer. Today it is most desirable – and may become even more so in the future – to expand a dancer's training and education far beyond these limits. Vocational students must also study various contemporary, jazz, historical and ethnic dance styles in order to become adequately trained dancers. They must be capable of satisfying the demands of a wide range of choreographers who will be creating new works in both classical and contemporary styles as well as reviving many of the old masterpieces for future audiences.

There were – and still are – a few examples during the period of advanced studies when one could teach two ballet systems and their styles with some success. Cecchetti and RAD systems were taught and examined with good results in the Royal Ballet School. In other vocational schools in Great Britain several ballet systems (ISTD, Legat, BBO, Russian, etc.) are still taught besides the above-mentioned syllabi. Giving students an opportunity to study a great variety of systems enables them to widen their perspectives and possibly attain a versatility of technique.

In the United States, Japan, and also in many European vocational schools, many teachers give daily practice in a more or less 'styleless' fashion. The classes are geared to gaining high-speed footwork, hyper-extensions, countless *pirouettes*, breathtakingly long balances on *pointes* and, of course, immense stamina. At the same time the classical head and arm movements are 'minimalised' and *barre*-exercises as well as centre *enchaînements* are mostly executed *en face*. The famous *épaulement*, which for a classical dancer – in my opinion – is 'not just a pretty position but a way of life', is hardly ever used.

One cannot help wondering if either of these solutions – the 'rich diet' of many systems and their styles, or the 'styleless style' method, might not result in producing dancers who achieve high standards in technique but lack the specific quality and style required not only from soloists but every group dancer, especially in those *corps de ballet* productions where a classical style is indispensable. One thinks of the group work in some nineteenth-century masterpieces – *La Bayadère, Swan Lake, Giselle, La Sylphide* – or those twentieth-century works created for classically trained dancers – Fokine's *Les Sylphides*, Balanchine's *Symphony in C*, Ashton's *La Valse*, Lander's *Etudes* and others. The essential value of the ensemble production in all these ballets depends on dancers with the special quality and style required by the choreography in question, who can also work together with absolute discipline, and keep their lines to perfection.

Experience has shown that from a quality and style point of view the best results were achieved in those ensembles where every dancer in the corps was trained in the same style for a long time.

To add to our difficulties concerning the purity of style, there is also a great need to teach daily classes in such a manner that students will become familiar with both the various styles of the nineteenth- and twentieth-century traditions and the greatly varied styles of those twentieth-century choreographers who were creating specifically for classically-trained dancers (from Fokine to Bintley by way of Balanchine, Massine, Tudor, Ashton, Petit, Cranko, MacMillan, Béjart, Van Manen, Neumeier, Robbins, Forsythe, et al.).

To find an answer to all these stressing problems we should look again at the **quality** of teaching, instead of trying to increase the **quantity** of ballet systems and styles taught to young ballet students.

Studying one good system thoroughly might fortify and crystallise students' techniques and their response towards quality and style. If students understand the importance of becoming pedantic in the one particular style they are regularly studying, they will become more responsive and caring about other styles when the opportunity arises.

Not so long ago a ballet company director needed extra

dancers for a new production of *Swan Lake*. She asked me to teach the final audition class for the few dancers she had already seen and selected.

'Do you want me to include in the class some *enchaînements* in a specific *Swan Lake* style?' I asked.

'No, I don't think there is any need for that – besides the usual requirements, I am mostly interested in these dancers' quality and style!' she answered.

Her words were music to my ears! Indeed, in a professional class one should be able to see whether a dancer has style aware-ness. She continued, 'If I can find dancers who have not only pleasing classical lines but who can also recognise the delicate nuances in quality and style, I'll have no difficulty in transforming them into swans or, for that matter, into anything else that our repertoire may require.'

I couldn't have agreed more with her opinion. However, there are sometimes special circumstances in the world of the theatre where even the daily classes can, and must, be co-ordinated with the current rehearsals with regard to style.

On another occasion I was invited to give daily classes for a ballet company and to coach the principals for a new choreo-graphic version of *Swan Lake*. This ensemble, including most of the principals, consisted mainly of rather young, but very talented, dancers. It was more than six years since Swan Lake had been in the company's repertoire – before the majority of these dancers became professionals – so they had never had a chance to learn, take part in, or even to see (except on video tape) any production of this masterpiece.

Understandably, direction and dancers were anxious to get the specific style right and it was my task to help them acquire and master this as fast as possible.

Everyone concerned knew that in these circumstances one can't accomplish all this through rehearsals only, so the daily practice also had to be used for this purpose. I realised that if we were to push this style down the dancers' throats relentlessly, for weeks on end, it would probably make them weary and irritated rather than interested, so I resolved to approach the task in an indirect way.

For the daily practice I decided not to give any *enchaînements* that were in the slightest way similar to any combination of steps in *Swan Lake*. I also asked the pianists not to play in class anything from Tchaikovsky's score. I tried to acquire the unique qualities of this specific style by giving the female dancers some exercises which would not only strengthen their backs but also make them more pliable. I demanded a lot of difficult and lengthy adages in which we concentrated on the lyrical and liquid quality of *port de bras* in general, and on harmonising the control and stamina of the most difficult movements with a softness and vulnerable femininity. However, we did all this without ever using any of the typical 'white swan' *port de bras*. In the *allegro* work we focused our attention on *épaulements* co-ordinated with a continuous flow of *petits ports de bras* executed with relaxed hands, fingers and necks.

I noticed that most of the male dancers lacked so-called 'royal, aristocratic manners' which, in this ballet, are absolutely essential. Many had difficulties with just walking in the right style – whether it was in the classical, *demi-caractère* or character roles. Therefore, the simplest walking and linking steps combined with discreet and noble arm gestures became regular elements within even the most complicated exercises. I also made sure in my classes that they didn't sacrifice the clarity of line, the clear directions, the simple and noble stance and hand-movement for the sake of virtuosity.

Working along these lines at classes seemed to pay dividends when we continued working in rehearsals to attain the required style and also when the premiere finally arrived.

It isn't only in theatrical life that classes can be used indirectly as suitable vehicles to educate dancers by implanting style awareness and to help them become finely attuned to the details that determine the different styles. Great care is needed as teachers can easily arouse or destroy their students' susceptibility towards different styles with their choice of music and its application in daily practice.

In Great Britain and the Commonwealth countries many teachers can make good use of the various 'purpose-composed' sets of music published by those organisations which create the syllabi. Though these are available in print, on disc and tape in most company-attached vocational schools and open classes (all over the world), there seems to be a preference for the use of 'free' music. Pianists may choose music according to their own taste, technique and what **they** believe would 'fit' the rhythm of the various *enchaînements* – from Bach to Honky-Tonky, from military marches to Chopin Impromptus, by way of Beethoven to Stravinsky and Gershwin and pop: tangos for *fondus*, fox-trots for *tendus*, and so on.

Admittedly, teachers and pupils find this more amusing and

refreshing – a very important factor in maintaining a good atmosphere in classes – rather than to listen, day after day, to the same syllabus score, however beautiful it may be! Regrettably, unless the choice of the accompanying music is done with a fairly good understanding of the actual period in ballet history (seldom the case where ballet pianists are concerned), a great variety of music in all kinds of style could become counter-productive as an accompaniment to class.

Instead of being helped and inspired by music composed by great musicians from the eighteenth and nineteenth centuries – the same periods from which the style of daily ballet classes is based – the dancers are accompanied mostly by music totally different to that style, or without any style at all. Students may become accustomed sub-consciously to ignoring the style and quality of the music played during their practice. When their teachers repeatedly remind them, 'For God's sake, listen to the music!' they will just make use of the beat they hear. To expect dancers to be musical in the real sense and sensitive to style, but at the same time to quasi-'immunise' them against being perceptive to music, is one of the great contradictions!

This unfortunate confusion can be remedied by guiding class pianists in their choice of music. The right application, chosen from the vast classical and romantic music repertoire, can play an important part in the process of implanting *style awareness*. It can also be used as an indirect, positive influence in making young dancers responsive to classical style.

Several courses of study in dancing and dance-related subjects – the history of art, music and dance, watching and analysing videos and live performances of the classics, classical mime and historical dancing – can help greatly in enhancing sensitivity to style. The most important support should come from repertoire classes *provided that* the chosen choreographies taught to the students are taken from a variety of periods and choreographers and it is essential that these carefully selected pieces are taught in the correct style by expert teachers.

All these lessons will help students assimilate the classical style as they are very closely linked to the daily technical ballet studies. Curiously enough, character dancing – often contrasted to classical dancing – is indirectly also a great help in developing an understanding of style differentiation. If the character teacher, besides teaching the steps and dances, also guides the students in their comprehension of how minor movement details – an inclination of the head, a wrist or elbow position, the focusing of the eyes, a certain stance, the degree of tilt of a torso, etc. – can change entirely the style and meaning of their dancing, they will learn to watch out for and recognise nuances of style. Once they learn to be observant in this direction there is good reason to believe that the process of implanting style awareness has been completed.

Spring cleaning

When students and professional dancers have been implanted with *style awareness* and are brought up to keep meticulously pure the classical style in their daily classes (whichever system they follow), they will become keenly observant of small details in other styles. Therefore it would be reasonable to expect that when it comes to working in a company the répétiteurs wouldn't need to worry too much about this aspect during rehearsals. Much precious time and energy are saved when working with dancers who have been brought up within the same system, particularly if their style is the same as that of the choreography being danced, e.g. Danish dancers rehearsing a Bournonville work or Kirov artists preparing a Petipa ballet.

Many ensembles, however, recruit dancers from all over the world, trained in different schools and all kinds of system. The greatest wish of most directors and choreographers is to find the ideal dancer for whom style, quality and technique are inseparable! If all these ideal individual dancers were schooled to become artists perceptive enough to recognise the fine details of style – in spite of their different training – then the task of the ballet master in unifying their various styles to the requirements of the given classical ballet would be so much easier and the production would have a far better chance of success. Alas, the reality is far from ideal, as a rule a greater part of rehearsal time has to be spent on trying to 'drill' the dancers into the necessary style.

A dancer's response to style can be enhanced by the right education but a true comprehension of style is an essential part of a dancer's artistic talent, a special gift, and some dancers happen to have more of it than others. It's not uncommon for répétiteurs to have to fight hard to attain the correct classical style in the *corps de ballet*, but with the leading dancers they should have little trouble. Nonetheless, répétiteurs often complain, 'They shouldn't be soloists if, at this stage of their career, they still need to be taught and corrected in the classical style! This is a waste of rehearsal time for everybody!'

There is some truth in these outbursts though they are the result of a form of 'professional sarcasm' to which overworked ballet masters are prone. However, this view that time spent on problems of style with soloists is unnecessary and a waste of energy can be counterproductive and it could lead to a situation where a rehearsal turns into a mere 'repeat and memorise' session where certain technical problems may be corrected, instead of a real preparation for an artistic and stylish performance.

To achieve the required standard répétiteurs may have to be pragmatic in appreciating the reality. Most companies have soloists who, as students, didn't receive enough correct tuition in the classical style and therefore lack *style awareness*, but they have attained their high ranking in the company through other merits – technical virtuosity, dramatic potential, excellent partnering. With proper understanding and patient coaching these artists can be guided to improve their sense of style.

A young principal, about to dance Albrecht for the first time, asked me to help him in the interpretation of the role. He had received his training in several systems, at different schools and companies, and worked with a number of famous teachers in Italy, the United States and Russia.

The technical execution of his solos was very sure and tidy and he danced them with ease and precision as well as in the right style. Obviously, wherever he had learned them, his repertoire teacher must have been very keen in imparting the purity of the right style to these solos. However, we soon found a few 'odd' situations as we worked on the rest of the role: problems arose in certain small details in the double-work, the way he related to his Giselle and in some of the mime scenes. An example of this occurred in the first act where Albrecht reaches out for Giselle's hand to prevent her going back into the house, pulls her gently away and then folds her arm into his.

Though the episode looked fresh and convincing as far as the meaning of the short scene was concerned, *the way* he touched and pulled Giselle's hand seemed to me to be out of style regarding the historical period at which the story takes place, the time when the ballet was choreographed, and the social background of the characters. The dancer's actions weren't exactly rough and his expression was loving and caring but it looked as if it was happening to any young couple of any social background in any everyday situation of today.

It didn't take us long to correct all these 'out of style' move-ments and manners throughout the ballet since he was an intelli-gent and talented dancer. Once I had pointed out to him a few of these problems, he began to recognise those critical moments during his dancing, walking, acting and reacting which he did in either a 'styleless' manner or in a false style. My corrections, combined with his own self-corrections, accelerated his progress in rehearsal and resulted in a very promising début.

It is even more difficult for some young principals to find the right style when they must perform a role from an old ballet in a new production where the choreography remains more or less unchanged but the story has been transplanted to a later period, even to the present day. On these occasions dancers may need a great deal of help in the rehearsals to find the right balance between the classical style of dancing and the period style of expressive gestures, mime scenes, and so on. The style of a simple walk on the stage may have to be changed completely according to the period and its costumes.

Even more careful considerations and changes of style are needed in those productions where not only the period but also the social background of the characters are changed significantly – Harlem Ballet's production of *Giselle* for example.

Ballet stars and leading dancers are often guests with a company, sometimes just for a few performances and occasionally for a longer period of time. Seldom do guests find that the style presented by the ensemble in their classical repertoire is identical with that in which they have been trained. This situation becomes even more compli-cated when more than one *étoile* happens to join the company at the same time. The 'stars' may well have been brought up in systems and styles entirely different from both those of the company and of one other, and be cast to dance in the same ballet, perhaps at the same performance, sometimes even as partners.

No matter how many world-famous stars are guesting with a company or how high their personal standards are, if they are dancing in styles different from the rest of the ensemble they usually cannot attain absolute satisfaction, even though their performances may have thrilling highlights. Guest artists and 'mega-stars' attract larger audiences – and greater box office returns – so one can understand why ballet companies invite inter-national ballet *étoiles* to please the public and solve their financial problems. But it has been shown that, in the life of those companies with great traditions, the less guest artists are involved the more a unity of style can be preserved.

Sadly, in the last few decades, both dancers and their audiences have become used to classical ballets being interpreted in a 'muddle' of styles, all over the world. Even more sadly, some members of the younger generation cannot even tell the difference!

Classicism in all art forms means perfect harmony, balance and unity of style. In classical ballet companies we can achieve this only through well-conducted rehearsals where the ballet master has to mould all members of the cast – including visiting artists – to dance, mime, act and react in the same style. This task often becomes almost impossible because of the pressures under which theatre managements and ballet artists are compelled to work today.

There is another important reason why, at rehearsals and company classes, ballet masters must keep their eyes on the purity of the classical style. Nowadays in most companies the wide range of repertoire requires classically trained dancers to master all kinds of different styles. To change from one style to another (sometimes within the same programme as is often the case in triple bills) is not easy and it demands tremendous concentration from the dancers. The task of remembering a vast chain of unaccustomed movements and their technical execution can become so complicated that under this special pressure the dancers' *style awareness* becomes temporarily suppressed and in some parts of the given choreography the unity of the particular style may suffer.

When classical dancers are working on modern creations one often hears the choreographer warning, 'Be careful not to look classical in this movement. . .' or 'Your arms should move with more weight, forget those airy classical *ports de bras*,' 'Less turn-out, please!' 'Let gravity do it!'

Dancers try their best to change their habitual classical style while learning and rehearsing a choreography created in a not strictly classical idiom. It is not surprising that, when they return to the classics, some contemporary manners might against their will, and perhaps only in the tiniest of details, affect the purity of their classical style. I was coaching a young ballerina for her début in *Giselle*. Her training, dramatic talent, sensitivity for style and her personality made her absolutely destined for the main role – it fitted her like a glove!

During the early rehearsals of the 'mad scene', it was obvious that she was capable of recreating in a very special way the tense atmosphere of the drama without over-acting. I welcomed the fact that, in spite of keeping tastefully to the traditional framework,

her interpretation took on an individual colouring. Her movements and facial expressions, as she gradually lost her senses, felt
strange, heard voices and had hallucinations, were so convincing
and touching to watch that it took me some while to free myself
from the emotional influence of her acting and to realise that there
was actually something which made me feel uneasy from a stylistic
point of view, though I couldn't put my finger on it at first. I had
to see her rehearsing it a few more times before I could put a name
to it – contemporary style. A few, hardly noticeable, but very
expressive images were influenced by contemporary techniques, a
fine mixture of the two styles – for example, a small shiver running
through her body and a crawling movement on the floor were each
emphasised by a slight contraction.

That this happened wasn't too surprising as this dancer
excelled in the works of such contemporary choreographers as
Christopher Bruce and Robert North, but it was essential that she
became aware of this mix of styles and correct it in time. By the
time of the performances her interpretation was not only touching
but in perfect style as well.

It often happens that young dancers in all ranks have to learn
roles from the old classical repertoire which are completely
unknown to them. It frequently occurs at short notice. In order to
save precious rehearsal time for other dancers and répétiteurs, as
well as studio space, these roles can be taught by choreologists or
dance notators with miraculous accuracy as far as step sequence
and musical counts are concerned.

In my experience if choreologists/notators are experts in their
own field and, at the same time, have the necessary background
and experience in conveying classical ballet excerpts with the
specific quality and style required, excellent results can be obtained
with this kind of coaching. Nevertheless, some of them don't have
enough dance experience in the field of classical ballet or they may
be lacking that special talent which helps to communicate quality
and style. In these emergency situations where a dancer has to go
on stage with only this kind of rapid coaching, the performance
will lack quality and style or become a real muddle of styles.

Mixing up styles is not only a problem for the young dancer or
principals making a début, it can happen to the more experienced
dancer, too.

A very famous ballerina wished me to rehearse her in the
leading role of *The Nutcracker*. As a young dancer she was
brought up in the Bournonville tradition and she had also the

benefit of studying the Vaganova system for many years with a world-famous representative of that method. She hadn't danced the role for quite a while but had no problem with technique or stamina. However, I was shocked to see how much polishing was needed to her interpretation with respect to style. She must have noticed that I was somewhat embarrassed when I frequently brought her attention to this fact.

'At the moment I am anxious to get the style of the ballet under my skin again. I am aware that there must be a lot to correct in this area as lately I have been dancing mostly a mixture of late twentieth-century works and the Bournonville repertoire, but hardly anything from Petipa. My brain remembers what the style should be like and if I watched somebody else dance it I would immediately recognise the 'out of style' images but, for the time being, my body is lost in a multitude of styles. I need a critical pair of eyes to guide me in this 'spring cleaning', and then, *it will be all right on the night!*'

I always recall her words when I come across similar situations in class or rehearsals, and when I am watching performances where the purity and consistency of the classical style are wanting.

If teachers in vocational schools would bring up their students in such a way that they become responsive to style, and if later when dancers, teachers, répétiteurs, choreologists and choreographers reproducing old productions of the classics would spend enough time and energy on 'spring-cleaning' with respect to style, then, indeed, one could always be sure that the style of each performance *would be all right on the night!*

❖

Repertoire

The influences of repertoire studies

When I was a young teacher, I was invited to attend the annual performance given by a well-established vocational school. The students' standard of dancing was generally very good, most of them performed with the charming freshness of youth and with an almost professional skill. The programme was constructed with good taste and consisted of some nicely arranged studies using classical ballet techniques, some choreographic pieces created specially for the occasion by the teachers and a guest choreographer which utilised character, contemporary, jazz and classical styles, and one *pas de deux* from the old classical repertoire.

There was a party after the performance where I met and talked with several of my colleagues most of whom shared my good opinion about the programme, but one of them, whose speciality was teaching the repertoire, had some reservations, 'I liked most of what I have seen but I think the programme was a bit unbalanced for a vocational school's annual display. Today we've seen the absolute minimum from the classical repertoire. It's unforgivable!'

'I agree that the show was lacking in this respect,' said another teacher, 'but, to be fair, there was so much more to show. . . you can't put on everything in a mere three hours, can you?'

'It's true,' interjected someone else, 'to be able to dance properly those compositions which are best known in the profession, is the real test. There are no easy ways to perform them as they were created for soloists! They are the best measure by which a student's technique, stamina, quality and style may be judged.'

A young teacher began to argue passionately, 'On these occasions I prefer to see students dancing arrangements which they are capable of performing well, instead of trying to dance some masterpieces inadequately. Performing 'made-to-measure' dances may be easier for the students and, of course, comparisons are out of the question, but in this way at least, both performers and the audience can genuinely enjoy themselves. I can't bear to see them ruining the classics.'

'Ruining?' queried the expert, much annoyed. 'If taught correctly students should be able to perform repertoire pieces without 'ruining' them at all. That is exactly my point!!!'

'Perhaps,' I ventured, 'it would have been more interesting to see more of the old and new repertoire performed in today's programme but their exclusion doesn't necessarily mean that this school's youngsters can't dance them properly.'

'Maybe I am a bit too suspicious when it comes to my subject,' admitted the 'expert'. 'If only I could be sure that every vocational school takes this matter as seriously as it deserves to be.'

I thought that he was over-dramatising a bit, not only for the given situation but the problem generally. Nevertheless, his words later influenced me enough to observe these issues in a different light and helped me understand through my own experiences that his concerns were not at all overstated.

Most of us in the profession would agree that for a dancer's all-round education it is invaluable to study the repertoire and perform items from it as much as possible. Regrettably it must be admitted that the majority of vocational schools all over the world – with very few exceptions – give an overwhelming priority to teaching technical classes and spend far less time and care on repertoire studies. Hence most dancers are not only ignorant of their artistic inheritance, and the riches of more contemporary creations, but they also lack the skill and culture to perform some of these masterpieces in the correct style of their given historical period as well as to interpret properly the differing personal characteristics of the various choreographers.

We all agree that the excperts taught from the repertoire should be chosen from a great variety of periods and choreographers in order to complete the students' knowledge and skills in the contrasting styles, and to enhance their own versatility but, in reality, this hardly happens anywhere.

In company-attached and other vocational schools where training is mainly classically orientated, the taught repertoire consists of a few well-known variations and *pas de deux*, mostly from the ballets of Marius Petipa (or his versions of other masters' choreographies which have since been lost – *Coppélia*, *Le Corsaire*, etc.) and, sometimes, students are taught a few additional excerpts from more recent works by the 'house' choreographer of the local company. (An exception is the Royal Danish Ballet School where repertoire from August Bournonville's ballets replaces that of Petipa.)

Generally studies are restricted to the style of one late nineteenth-century choreographer with little else from the earlier part of that century or even from the huge variety of styles, and choreographers, of the twentieth century. Sadly, there are few fragments reconstructed from creations of the eighteenth century and earlier, but it is regrettable that these rare treasures of our traditions remain almost completely unknown to most of today's young dancers.

Those vocational schools which prepare pupils for a career in musical theatre or specialise in contemporary dance hardly ever have the opportunity to raise their students' classical technique to a level which would enable them to perform the majority of the above-mentioned repertoire authentically – particularly as far as *pointe*-work, *batterie*, multiple *pirouettes, tours en l'air, manèges*, etc. are concerned. These students are unable to learn a greater part of their artistic inheritance through physical experience but that should not stop them from becoming better educated and understanding and appreciating their artistic roots, without which no creative and interpretative artist's training can be called complete. After all, most learned musicians - even if they have specialised in contemporary or jazz music - have studied their classical traditions.

It is possible to select carefully several sections from classical ballets which could be taught to these pupils without causing physical damage or sacrificing the authenticity of the original choreography. The students would benefit and have the pleasure of learning the numerous mime parts, character dances and *corps de ballet* sections for soft shoes or character boots from the best of our traditions – *Giselle, Coppélia, The Nutcracker, Napoli, La Sylphide*, as well as *The Sleeping Beauty, Don Quixote* and *Raymonda*, to name but a few.

Apart from these specific repertoire lessons, students of music theatre and contemporary dance could also benefit from watching video tapes of classical ballet productions under the tutelage of an expert teacher to analyse these creations from the point of view of structure, style and interpretation. These studies would help them to broaden their horizons, make them more knowledgeable, cultured and critical about their own area within the art of dance, and it may also contribute a great deal to their future activities of choreography and improvisation.

There are quite a few vocational schools where the training geared to producing contemporary dancers or music theatre artists, misses out not only on the classical repertoire but students often are also deprived of the benefits of regular repertoire classes in which they could be taught many pieces from the vast choice of modern works choreographed in the differing contemporary styles.

Whichever type of vocational school's programme one investigates, one finds in most cases that there is not enough time, emphasis or variety given for teaching from the repertory. This situation gives cause for great concern.

The topic of 'why', 'what', 'when' and 'how' to teach the repertoire came up in a lively discussion after a lecture I gave to professional dancers on a teachers' training course.

'When I was a student,' said one of them, 'our teachers took these studies very seriously. I had no doubt that what I gained through them was going to be most useful for my career, but after joining a classical company it didn't take long for me to find out that most of it was just a waste of precious time and energy!'

'Why was that?'

'When you are in the *corps de ballet* you hardly need any knowledge of how to dance the variations and *pas de deux* which we studied in those lessons – they are created for soloists and principals.'

'True,' agreed another participant, 'perhaps if we had practised the *corps de ballet* choreography from *La Bayadère*, *Giselle* or *Swan Lake* and the like we would have had a much better preparation for handling the real challenges in the first year of life in a company – specially for those dancers who might well stay in the *corps* for good. It would have meant a solid support for their entire professional life. How to relate to each other, how to work in line, how to keep distances when dancing within a group; these are the skills young dancers should know when joining a company.'

'Well, those famous variations I was taught as a student,' remarked a young man, 'didn't help me much when I became a soloist either and started rehearsing some of the classical roles.'

'Why? Did your memory fail you?'

'No. I remembered quite easily what I had learnt at school but having a good memory was more often a 'pain in the neck' because many of the versions we had been taught differed from the ones danced in my company's productions. It would have been much better and faster to learn the choreography from scratch than to keep altering one's memories. However, that wasn't the real problem. The root of my troubles wasn't embedded in what I did learn at those repertoire classes but in what I didn't! It seems that the only knowledge I picked up was no more than a miserable 'order of steps' as they appeared in the choreography and – if and when I was lucky enough to have the required technique for them – to execute them properly. . .'

'You aren't fair,' interjected someone, 'if nothing else, you gained performing stamina during those lessons.'

'As a dancer yourself,' he answered, 'you don't need me to tell you that the real performing stamina should come from daily classes and performance on stage; repertoire classes should offer you something extra!'

'Learning authentic choreography and its technical execution should be enough of a reason for which to be grateful,' was someone else's reaction. 'Why do you belittle these results?'

'Because, when it comes to the 'proof of the pudding', all these achievements turned out to be of little use to me. The moment I danced these excerpts on the stage, my aim couldn't be just the execution of a sequence of steps, no matter how correct technically or with what endurance I have managed. For me – and I believe for most soloists – the real challenge has to be in the re-creation of the role and then the task of becoming one and the same with it in characterisation, period and the style of the choreography.'

'That's exactly what I meant,' said the girl who originally started this argument, 'when I referred to the 'waste of time and effort' in the repertoire classes we did at school. I am sure that for a young performing artist to interpret even the smallest of roles with the quality required by any of the classical or contemporary masterpieces, there needs to be taught a great deal more than, with due respect, the authentic order of steps!'

Everything that was said made me think again, though my own experiences as a dancer and teacher convinced me that repertoire classes could be the most important influence in a dancer's mental and emotional development, and I believe that they should not be considered as time-wasting but given all possible support. However, there is an urgent need to reconsider how we might achieve this.

One day the director of a vocational school asked me to coach some students in a few classical variations which were to be danced in a forthcoming performance. 'You needn't waste time teaching them the steps, they already know them. What they need from you are style, refinement and performing skills. . .'

I was relieved to note that the technical demands of the chosen variations were not beyond the students' capabilities so there was no danger of either harming their physiques or distorting the choreography. (Regretfully, such things do often happen at annual school displays, summer courses, seminars and the like.)

Most of the solos were from *The Sleeping Beauty*, amongst them that in the last act generally known as 'Florestan's Sister's variation'. The girl chosen to dance it had the musicality and the footwork needed to perform it but she found it difficult to dance at the correct speed and co-ordinating the sharp *batteries* and *pointe*-work with the busy *ports de bras* which are not typical 'class-room' ones. I thought to help her by finding some meaning to the role and engaging her imagination and emotions more.

'Originally this solo was called 'Gold' – one of the four different precious metals and gems given as presents to the just-married couple. The music and choreography were meant to convey the jingling and brightness of this valuable metal. When you are dancing it you mustn't think of it as a 'tricky' and impossibly fast task, instead you should transform yourself into a shiny coin – desirable but hard to catch! Imagining this will encourage you to achieve all the speed and co-ordination you need. Listen to the tinkling of the percussion in the orchestration, that will help you perform with lightness and rapidity. Have you heard the full score?'

'No, I haven't.'

Suddenly, I suspected that wasn't the only question I should ask. Maybe there was a lot more these students didn't know about the ballet.

'Do you know who composed the music?'

Embarrassment and surprise were written on their faces. There was no answer. 'Who choreographed these excerpts you are learning?' elicited a guess from one girl, 'Petipa?' My last desperate enquiry, 'In which century was it created?' brought forward the proud answer from one of the boys, 'The late eighteenth!!!'

Afterwards, I found out that neither teachers nor students were to be blamed. The pupils' ignorance was due to a simple fact: the two subjects were not co-ordinated, as the dance-history lessons had not yet reached beyond the early eighteenth century.

Another time two young professionals asked me to help them with the 'Blue Bird' *pas de deux* and variations. They were to dance it at short notice. As I was not familiar with their company's production, I asked the girl, 'Are you a bird or a princess in your version?'

'Oh! I am afraid I don't know. We are both new to the company and it wasn't mentioned in rehearsals. We just learnt the steps very quickly, you know how it is at a time of crisis. . .'

'Yes, but you should have asked. For Heaven's sake, how will you perform the role if you don't even know whether you are supposed to behave, move and react as a little bird or as a princess?'

'Oh dear, this is the first time I heard that this part can have different interpretations. Why didn't I know? Why didn't I ask?'

Why, indeed. . .?

As repertoire studies play a vitally important role in a dancer's artistic development, and as time and energy factors are always too pressing in our work, it seems worthwhile to clarify those unique values offered by repertoire studies – characterisation, expressive interpretation, performing skills, style studies of the different periods as well as the various choreographers. By concentrating on these aspects – and leaving other beneficial factors (technique, stamina, memorising, musicality, dance history) to be taken care of in other technical and academic studies – and by making sure that repertoire lessons are always harmonised with the current technical and academic standards of the students, our efforts are bound to result in an 'artistic bonus'. With less time and energy spent we could perhaps get closer to the final goal: to educate dancers in such a way that it will be a second nature for them to want to find some meaning to every role they perform, and at the same time achieve their wish that each interpretation should become strongly individual.

Has the Magic Gone?

The dancer as a creative artist

It is clear that technical standards in dance are at present generally impressive worldwide, while in the past that was true for only a few companies. Because of higher and healthier living standards, better education and medical care, improved facilities such as flooring, heating, more suitable shoes and dancewear, most dancers have a chance to receive an improved training and to cultivate better-proportioned and highly capable bodies. These are more sensitively tuned with better-shaped muscle structures, higher extensions, and a greater strength and endurance than in previous times. Then, dancers needed to perfect themselves in only a few disciplines and styles (classical ballet, character and mime), whereas today they are trained to cope with numerous additional dance techniques and choreographic styles which didn't exist in the past.

On the stage, more than ever before, 'high-tech' machinery and lighting can help our generation of dancers immensely in creating magical theatrical effects, as does the use of more sophisticated and imaginative textiles for costumes.

As a result, today's choreographers have all the facilities to hand for revitalising the 'magic' of the classics and making them look more interesting than when they were premiered. When composing new works they can choreograph as freely as their fantasy takes them, with daring and intricacy. Some dancers and choreographers make the best of these given opportunities and this results in pleasurable productions and occasionally, new masterpieces.

However, when assessing the present situation as a whole, one cannot help having mixed feelings. There are many performances where one feels that there is a lot on offer but something important is missing. One may be well entertained, and often dazzled, by the virtuosity of certain dancers or impressive stage effects, but one is not touched. It is as if there was no real substance to the dance;

nothing to involve either the dancers or the audience in a truly
artistic experience. These performances lack that 'magical' atmosphere which is the essence of all interpretative art forms, and
which has been experienced so often in the past. Why has this
'magic' disappeared?

Good performances are given by artists with strong personalities, but magical ones can be generated only when the performing creativity of a charismatic leading dancer is matched by an
ensemble of performers with a prominent stage presence.

Why is it that in spite of all the advances in the dance profession, and the talent of the numerous youngsters who enter
vocational schools each year, dancers have become stereotypes
instead of charismatic individuals? Why is it that we can produce
dancers of versatility, virtuosity and with beautiful physiques but
artists such as those of the past, 'legends in their own time', rarely
ever emerge today?

In recent years these questions often crossed my mind, but were
my doubts justified? Since I became an 'aged' professional I have
been afraid that I might be falling into the usual habit of looking
at the past through rose-tinted spectacles while seeing all the faults
of the present greatly enlarged under a microscope.

Was I glorifying and enshrouding in mystique our yesterdays
while criticising today too harshly? Was I becoming a grumbling,
embittered old professional, a dated and sour ex-dancer, secretly
jealous of youth? As I have always despised this kind of person I
have closely scrutinised my responses and came to the conclusion
that this was not the case.

I gradually became aware that many people of all age groups –
dancers, and others from within the profession as well as the
public – felt similarly to myself. We all seemed to be greatly
disturbed that our art form has lately changed: extreme physical
accomplishment overshadows true artistic quality. A result of this
is an excessive lack of strong personalities on the stage.

I believed that part of the problem might stem from the physically minded methods by which young candidates are often
selected for entry into vocational schools and for later professional
life (I have already discussed these issues in 'Survival of the Fittest'
and 'Glass or Diamond'), and some attitudes towards teaching and
auditions which damage a dancer's self-confidence. However, I
didn't think these to be the **only** reasons.

At the same time I noticed that similar symptoms occurred in
other art forms. Teachers of singing and music, coaches and critics,

are also worried that too many of the new generation of singers and musicians are becoming perfect robots, combining 'devilish' skills and virtuosity with enormous stamina, instead of trying to discover their own identity and an individual sound.

There must be a common reason causing this artistic decline in all these art forms.

Artists usually react sensitively to the trends of their times and, even if they wished to, they wouldn't be able to detach themselves completely from the idols and ideologies of their surrounding society.

The twentieth century has produced modern versions of the Golden Calf – combustion engines, cameras, cinema, hi-fi, TV and video, telephones and other communication systems, etc. Above all *computers* have become our idols. We have created them for our pleasure and comfort, to own, use and enjoy, not to be feared. They are the result of man's ambition and the proof of a human's capacity to achieve a higher quality of life through technical precision.

We live in an absolutely technically minded and materialistic society where the motivating force is to challenge and outdo any measurable achievement. Translated into dance terms this means more *pirouettes*, higher extensions, greater speed, loftier jumps, a faster transfer of weight, increasingly intricate rhythmical and dynamic challenges with quicker changes of direction and more complicated double-work, and so on. The wish to fulfil these tasks is natural and exciting for most dancers. It has always been the ambition for each generation of young artists to challenge and possibly overtake the technical prowess of its predecessors as well as present rivals. These are positive aims and there is nothing wrong with them as long as they don't become the **only** goal as far as their vocation is concerned.

To be appreciated and admired by the public has always been one of the driving forces of an interpretative artist. Perhaps today's young artists sub-consciously feel the only way to be appreciated and admired by their technically minded audiences is to try to overwhelm them with something measurable, to outshine the intricacy, precision and capacity of those man-made machines which are their common idols.

In order to accomplish this goal during the short period of their dancing life, it seems that dancers engage so much time as well as physical and mental energy, that there is hardly any chance left for them to seek, find and establish their own artistic identity through dancing. By the time their personality has matured, the body will be too tired to support the metamorphosis from a skilled crafts-man to a real artist.

If this is the case, do we just submissively watch this infectious trend pass by, eradicating – like an epidemic – most of the values which differentiate art from craft? Can we afford to let the 'magic' go? The obvious answer to these dramatic questions can be nothing else but: NO! NEVER!

Those of us who see this corrupt trend as being alarming should look for some remedy which might stop this contagious disease before dancing becomes more and more estranged from its artistic values and converts into some kind of sophisticated athletic enter-tainment. But how, and where, can we seek this 'magical remedy'?

The solution may not be easy, or rapid, but it might turn-out to be more simple and closer than one would imagine; one may find the key is in our own hands – teachers', dance-aesthetes' and critics'.

In a review of a young and promising ballerina's début in *Les Sylphides*, a critic praised her technique, style, musicality and quality, and he foresaw a great future for her. He compared her interpretation to that of the legendary Alicia Markova and found that it was close, but not yet the same. Other complimentary write-ups by different critics in the press also found it praiseworthy that this young ballerina should emulate her illustrious predecessor in her manners, style and interpretation.

The review gave the impression that any slight deviations in the interpretation were only because of the difference in age and experience of the two artists. No doubt maturity and experience play an important role in an artistic interpretation, but don't such comments disregard anything about what the individuality and stage personality of a dancer actually mean? Why should a talented dancer strive to become a precise replica of someone else? Could any two great artists be exactly the same? If this were true wouldn't it be artistically negative and boring for both dancers and audience?

In making such comparisons, well-meaning critics can often unwittingly lead young dancers to copy some of the greatest personalities in the dance world instead of encouraging them just to learn from them and then seek out their own identity.

We teachers often make the same mistakes when we teach repertoire in vocational schools or when coaching young artists for company performance in certain roles associated with other noted dancers. We may unintentionally frighten them away from bringing any individuality to their performance by coaching them to dance in the manner of one of our own great idols. Can we recognise the subtle difference between preparing dancers for an interpretation which is true to the traditions of the style of the choreographer and period, through an individual artist's personality, or trying to replicate the mannerisms of an unique personality? Don't we often suppress the living creativity of an interpretative artist for the sake of copying the dead?

Brilliant, unforgettable performances were, and are, given because of a particular dancer's individual approach, charisma, physique and talent. Surely, these are the qualities we should look for and enhance in a promising dancer.

I may also say that trying to be different for its own sake is just as bad as trying to imitate another's personality. Both of these tendencies lead dancers to perform with a personality not their own and their portrayals will be false.

At a rehearsal of William Dollar's ballet *Le Combat*, the heroine, Clorinda, was danced by one of the company's leading ballerinas with a refined and uniquely touching interpretation. The 'second cast' dancer was studying her in the background. Afterwards the répétiteur asked the ballerina to demonstrate a few of the tricky bits which had caused some problems for the new cast. When this demonstration had finished the répétiteur proceeded to give further corrections to the understudy.

'Watch every little detail! I want you to do it **exactly** as she does, it is so beautiful. . . but, oh dear, you are doing it so differently. . .' Turning to the ballerina, he continued, 'Please, would you show her your death scene; when the crusader discovers he has fought a duel with a woman in disguise and where you synchronise your vivacious gestures of 'wanting-to-hide-the-truth' with the vague, soft movements of a weakening body of a dying girl. . .'

In his enthusiasm the répétiteur didn't realise that his praise wasn't bringing about the expected effect. The more vividly he described the details of the ballerina's individual interpretation, the more uneasy the atmosphere became. Both dancers found it difficult to hide their irritation.

After the répétiteur had left, the ballerina told me in confidence, 'This ballet was originally created for Janine Charrat. Unfortunately, I never saw her legendary interpretation and her physique and mentality were quite different from mine, so our performances must have differed. Considering the fame and charisma of that original cast I should be flattered that my portrayal is valued so highly, but I have mixed feelings. Somehow there seems to be a contradiction. I am told that I manage to create something artistic with this role; in other words I perform it in an individual way. If so, it should be respected as such by marking it with my 'copyright', instead of trying to 'photocopy' it. I hope this doesn't sound too pompous or jealous. What I am trying to say is that, after learning the choreography of a role, dancers should re-create it according to their own personality. Actually, neither dancer nor audience gains much when performers copy or are copied.'

It often happens that younger dancers are coached by artists who themselves danced – or are still dancing – the role in question. This is usually a most professional learning process and has excellent results, especially when the coach has the ability to convey and correct, and has the patience to bring to the surface the youngster's personality. However, there are many cases when the coach's forceful or possessive disposition, enthusiastic impatience suppresses the artist's as yet unformed identity.

Many youngsters lament, 'My coach is a wonderful dancer and I am very lucky to learn from such an experienced artist. But, when I hear all the time 'I danced it this way' and 'this is how you must also do it' I feel suffocated because I can't use my initiative. I don't want to dance like somebody else. I need to find my own way. I WANT TO BE ME!'

Young artists at the beginning of their careers, are always inclined to fall into the habit of emulating some of their idols, even without any encouragement from over-enthusiastic mentors. Dancers want to live up to the traditions and highly valued standards of the ballet stars of yesteryear.

With the assistance of modern technology the opportunity to copy others has become much easier, and the temptation much greater, than in the past. Just as musicians and singers can listen to, and reproduce, other artists' interpretations from discs and tapes, dancers can study from a vast choice of video-taped performances of eminent dancers. Slow-motion reveals even more! Young and ambitious dancers can easily become overwhelmed by such brilliant and charismatic performers, so much so that, instead of just learning from them, they will simply imitate them without bringing their own personality to the surface.

I was watching a rehearsal, conducted by one of the most loved and experienced coaches of all time, at which a charming soloist was preparing for her début as Aurora. From every point of view she was suited to this task. Yet, something was wrong. Everything she created seemed to consist of carefully studied images which were alien to her own personality. Her otherwise fresh girlishness changed into an affectation. It was obvious that she was copying the ways of her great idol, the company's leading ballerina.

'You could be a delightful Aurora,' the coach said to her, 'if you would allow yourself to become just her, instead of being busy fitting into someone else's unique performing manner. Copying it makes you look like a counterfeit. Let your personality form your own Aurora, then you will be charming and convincing.'

What a wonderful and sincere coach he was! His wise words helped me to understand for the rest of my career that if criticism, teaching and coaching are inspired by the principal idea of interpretation being a creative art and not a skill of clever imitation, then dancers will develop into charismatic personalities.

In the last part of the twentieth century people's life-style, trends, tastes and ideology have changed beyond recognition and teaching techniques in every art form must follow suit. If we seek out different ways and attitudes in our methods of teaching and rehearsing, we may succeed better in nurturing more 'unique' individuals who, besides an impressive technique, have the 'magic power' to create unforgettable performances.

By re-establishing in young dancers' minds the importance of quality, style, musicality, personal refinements and, first and foremost, their own individual interpretation in dancing, we might stop the spread of an 'epidemic' which diverts our muse, Terpsichore, from her real worth and reach again the 'magical' values of past performances, perhaps even surpassing them.

❖

Comparisons

A dancer's development as compared with that of other performers

Dancers are easily persuaded by their older colleagues that their professional life and problems are so special it is pointless to compare them with the circumstances of any other performing artist.

Failing to make a comparison between their own aspirations, fights, failures and achievements and those of their siblings is counter-productive and could result in the dancer's horizon becoming greatly restricted. They will become resigned and quiescent beings, believing that everything in their little world will remain unaltered. This leads dancers into childish helplessness and a meek passivity, a behaviour which might suit some short-sighted or autocratic company directors but could inhibit the development of an interpretative artist. That is why dancers – specially those spending their active life in lyric theatre ensembles – easily find themselves somewhat isolated and often pitied, snubbed or even humiliated by the rest of the artistic world. None of this helps to build the self-respect and confidence which is a fundamental condition for everyone.

Instead of shrinking from comparisons, dancers – and specially teachers – should study in detail how artists who work in other interpretative art forms deal with almost identical difficulties. From these observations they could adapt a good many ideas about how to apply some of the better methods to enhance progress in our particular art form.

It might be worthwhile discovering which of our siblings suffer most from the decay caused by the 'pigeon-hole' system and the influence of dated and preconceived ideas from an early age.

Perhaps one should start the comparison with musicians, as they are the only other performing artists who – apart from dancers – have to train from early childhood and need to develop that strict discipline which enables them to perform in groups.

Whilst dancers study regularly in large groups and often with different teachers, music students work with their mentors for many years on the basis of an intimate 'one-to-one' ratio. Being taught individually over such a span the changing and developing personalities of the youngsters can be closely watched and served by their teachers according to each individual's specific need. Observing the pupils' personal inclinations, special talents and possible imperfections teachers may guide the young musicians towards a wider horizon rather then labelling them and restricting their development.

Students are coached through the vast repertoire of music in great detail and in the various styles of composers from different periods. (Much more time and emphasis is given to this part of their studies than any dance student receives for period studies and differentiation between the personal styles of various choreo-graphers.) Instead of denying certain students the possibility of success in the interpretation of this or that style (unfortunately, often the case in dancers' vocational schools) music teachers demand from all their pupils demonstrations of intelligence and refinement in each style, at exams as well as during school concerts. In this way musicians have numerous opportunities during their student years to study thoroughly and then work to show in actual performances the kind of individual interpretation of which they are capable – even in those styles which, in their teachers' opinion, do not match their personality or for which they are not yet mature enough.

Whatever teachers' opinions may be about the artistic make-up of some of their students, their 'pigeon-hole' labelling will have little consequence on the future of their graduates because – in contrast with the dancers' vocational schools – none of the music academies is attached to any of the professional orchestras. When young musicians seek engagements they are auditioned by experts who are independent – therefore uninfluenced by the opinions of the candidates' previous teachers or school directors.

After leaving school and throughout their careers, musicians continually have the chance to study and perfect themselves in any style, period and composer they wish to perform. Most musical scores are easily accessible from various libraries so they can make a profound investigation of any composition and learn to play it in their own time. Recording it for later analytical playback and correction is a simple way to lead them on to critical self-discovery.

At present most of these ideal situations are unimaginable for dancers. Very few of them are taught to read any of the existing notation systems, nor are there enough adequately notated scores of older ballets as they were originally created, or in the way they have been reproduced since. Videotapes of new productions of the classics and contemporary creations are so few and new to the scene that they can hardly fill the gap. Besides the luxury of suitable studio space, time and musical accompaniment, dancers would need a répétiteur or notator (all of these, if available, costing a fortune!) to accomplish even the smallest role in the dance repertoire. At present dance schools and companies cannot afford to own enough essential video-recording equipment and it is out of the question for every student and dancer to have individual use of these expensive tools for the sake of exploration and self-discovery.

When freelance musicians audition for a job, or members of an orchestra aspire for promotion, they are listened to individually by a distinguished panel of professionals. They have the chance to play various solos of their own choice as well as those required by the auditioning committee. These are occasions when musicians have an opportunity to show their superiors that they are not limited to certain styles, periods and composers but are able to play to the required standards all kinds of music which may be included in the orchestra's present and future repertoire. Because of the musicians' all-round training most of them are able to demonstrate their versatility as well as their outstanding qualities. Decisions about their future will be taken on merit, good work and progress.

For a dancer a similar situation would be a 'pipe dream' rather than a well-tried routine. At open auditions – aptly nicknamed 'cattle markets' by angry and humiliated dancers – they are seen only in a crowded class and are rarely given a chance to dance a classical variation or a modern piece.

In school-attached companies the auditioning system varies according to local tradition. However, the outcome will usually be much influenced by the opinions of the school director and teachers, even where the artistic direction of the company is not identical to that of the school.

The position of solo concert performers is very different from that of orchestral members. It is entirely up to their own artistic conviction as to what type of programmes they choose to present to their audiences at the different stages of their career. In contrast to prominent leading dancers, it is taken for granted that outstanding musicians can and do take responsibility for their artistic decisions, though they may take into consideration the advice given by others – experts, agents, critics and impresarios – whose opinions they can respect. They have the freedom to perform all kinds of composition according to their own convictions, even if these have been performed by other distinguished artists in very different styles, tempi and sound quality.

To be allowed to perform according to one's own choice, taste, imagination and feelings, and letting the audience be the sole judge about it, is a marvellous way to make an art form progress. How exciting it must be for the public to listen to and compare different artists interpreting the music of, say, Bach and to follow the arguments and verifications of the different interpretations.

Musicians, rightly or wrongly, are often breaking traditional rules, showing a composition in a different light or pointing out the misconceptions of some past performers. Through these processes their public is able better to understand and appreciate music, its history and such things as authenticity. The more knowledgeable the audience becomes the better taste it will develop, thus it will become a serious, critical body demanding high artistic standards from the artists. Can anyone better serve an art form, and shouldn't similar circumstances prevail in the world of Dance?

With the exception of a handful of 'mega' ballet stars, which of our leading artists – particularly ballerinas and principal male dancers – could dare to dream of a situation in which they could have their own say about the type of roles they feel they are suited to, and capable of performing, what they should or shouldn't dance, and in what manner?

On the presumption that 'dancers haven't got the slightest self-knowledge' they are neither consulted nor given any explanation as to why they are not cast in certain roles. The allegation that dancers – unlike their siblings – are incapable of recognising their own potential and skills is arrogant and humiliating, though there may be some truth in it. However, the prevalent 'pigeonhole' system doesn't exactly help an artist to become aware of his or her true and complex inner self!

Leading artists may have a certain position in which they are supposed to represent their company and art form at a top level but often they don't receive permission to learn and rehearse at least some roles which they consider they could develop to a high standard. Without a répétiteur, a studio and plenty of rehearsal time, dancers cannot learn any role – let alone develop and mould it to their own personality. They have no chance to show either to themselves, a director or other official what they feel they are capable of doing. This is hardly the best way to find self-identity and gain self-knowledge! Also members of the audience are deprived of judging for themselves whether the artist's individual interpretation in a specific role would be pleasing or not, so their knowledge of dancing remains limited and their taste is influenced by the company director's casting policy which is often based on preconceived ideas. . .

One can't help concluding that the systems by which musicians nurture their young talents and respect their more mature artists during their careers are not only very different but far superior to ours. But what about actors and opera singers? What is their situation in comparison with musicians or are these particular siblings `wearing the same outdated and uncomfortable shoes' as dancers?

All these interpretative artists have a common element in that their vocation is to convey to the public creations by various authors in different historical periods. Excepting musicians, their artistry also involves characterisation on the stage and their progress greatly depends on how they are cast in different roles, and the tools of their artistic creativity are not sophisticated instruments made from a variety of fabrics but their own bodies and vocal attributes.

In a dancer's case, physical capability, appearance and the proportions of the body strongly influence the choice of roles for which they will be cast from the point of view of quality and style. Actors rely on their voices as well as their facial and general appearance; for singers the range, colour and volume of their vocal resources determine in which category they will be placed. As common factors might produce more or less identical situations one would expect that actors, singers and dancers would equally suffer from the 'pigeonhole' system of casting. But do they?

A great number of dancers are trained in company-connected schools so, unavoidably, the procedure of being 'labelled' will start from childhood. As company personnel are usually in close contact with the school's staff – often working at the school as well – graduating dancers can hardly ever shake off the stigma received as immature students, which may influence – rightly or wrongly – their future career in the company.

For a few dancers the situation may alter with a change of director (whose tastes may be different), or when a guest choreographer or répétiteur takes on the sole responsibility for casting. In both circumstances the choice of dancers for the various roles will depend on experts using a fresh vision and therefore is not influenced by preconceived ideas. However, for practical reasons the latter situation occurs but rarely. There is seldom enough time for outside choreographers to become familiar with the talents of all the dancers in a company so they will have to rely upon information and recommendations provided by the artistic direction. It is also true that few guest artists would wish to create difficulties with the director of their host company; they would prefer to be diplomatic and remain on friendly terms with the direction. Notwithstanding, when professionalism prevails, guest choreographers and répétiteurs often help to discover hidden talents within a company.

The other way for frustrated dancers to leave behind this syndrome of type-casting is to change companies. However, most dancers – unless they are already principals – are hesitant to choose this option for several reasons. Being brought up in the vocational school not to act or think for themselves they lack the confidence and independence to leave the organisation and the familiar people in it, a home and family to them since childhood. They are afraid to face up to new challenges amongst 'strangers'.

Apart from feeling unsafe, dancers also suffer a kind of shame: they have grown up with the idealisation of their own establishment so leaving it would mean an admission of their own failure. Being aware of the very short span of their professional lives they tend to panic from the mere thought of losing precious time in trying to re-establish themselves, finding a suitable partner and learning a new repertoire in an unfamiliar company. Though feeling frustrated and disillusioned they still may prefer to carry on in the hope of some lucky change. Those dancers of less sensitivity may just resign themselves to the situation with a cynical view: 'Better the devil you know. . .' and – though unhappy and unfulfilled – they compromise by staying where they are.

How can we expect more quality, sensitivity, imagination and creativity – the real criteria of artistry – in an art form where so many of the artists who create it have to build on submission, frustration, unhappiness and cynical compromise as a foundation for their professional activity?!

From the start, young actors – and singers – are in a far better situation. Serious training can start only at a more mature age and their vocational schools are independent of theatre companies and opera houses. It is less likely that teachers' type-casting – if any – would influence their opportunities. When auditioning for a play, opera or musical they will be judged, chosen and cast by the results of thorough auditions at which they must perform several roles in character and various excerpts from a wide range of repertoire, at a more mature age. Becoming successful in a specific role may result in type-casting but actors and singers have ample time and opportunity during their active lives to rid themselves of the 'pigeonhole' into which they have been forced, unless some of them become members of the few existing permanent repertory companies. They have a fair chance to prepare and prove their artistic versatility, as well as the stronger and more valuable features of their personality, on many occasions and at all stages in their career, and to several experts in their respective professions.

Amongst interpretative artists – apart from musicians – perhaps actors have the best chance for changing from time to time their 'unwanted' labels. With a long artistic lifespan, an advanced system of auditions and the vast opportunities given by television, film, radio, video and puppetry, as well as numerous theatre productions, they have little to lose by changing from one engage-ment to another – unlike dancers. They will gain much experience as well as break through prejudiced opinions. It has often happened that a comedian becomes a serious actor; a classical actress takes a part in a musical or a comedy; the type-cast villain plays the role of the innocent hero – or vice-versa. Sometimes these experiments may turn-out to be mistakes – in which case they may give those artists better self-knowledge – but without taking some risks these performers would be depriving their public of those numerous successful changes which become fresh artistic interpre-tations.

If only some similarly inspiring experiences could enrich the dance world! Unfortunately, audiences and artists are rarely granted this pleasure as dancers, particularly those in classical companies, are cast during their entire performing life according to the old label received when they were juveniles.

Because of the nature of the art form, no other performing artist is so defenceless against type-casting as the opera singer. They are categorised into limited role-playing more or less right from the start of their studies. While they concentrate on the general technique of singing, it is the range, quality, volume and colour of the voice which determine how their training should be accomplished from the beginning. Teachers will advise them in which range (tenor, baritone, bass, etc.) the voice will best excel, and then will come that extra 'labelling' within these categories (lyrical, dramatic, buffo, etc.). Additionally they must foresee whether the student is more suited to an Italian, French, Russian or German repertoire or perhaps has gifts more appropriate for operetta or musical theatre.

The system puts a great deal of responsibility upon the tutors, though their opinion will be tested further and, if necessary, amended, as each individual's personality, characteristics of the voice and acting ability become manifest. A singer's studies take place during early adulthood and are established on a 'one-to-one' basis. Artists will be prepared for a specific repertoire (suited for their particular voice range) as well as their overall personal make-up. Because of the exceptional comprehension under which a singer's training takes place, one hears only occasionally of a young artist's vocal range or capacity being initially misjudged. In most cases correction is possible by resting the voice and then re-training it. The possibilities of making a crucial and irreversible error through misdirecting a student singer are far less than during a dancer's vocational training which begins at a time when body and personality are as yet unformed and where the daily training takes place in large groups and is mostly generalised instead of 'made-to-measure'.

Although opera singers are in danger of being categorised, their situation is far better than a dancer's. They are adults at a time when specialisation is applied. Their given specialist 'label' is not so much a stigma for life but more a helpful 'ticket' towards a success-ful career. If they are given a wrong 'ticket' to a false 'destination', singers – unlike dancers – are able, during their longer career, to alter an incorrect direction mistakenly given by their teacher.

This brief comparison between educational systems for musicians, actors, singers and dancers offers a great number of recommendations for radical changes and improvements in the education of dancers.

These changes should take place both at student level and during dancers' professional careers.

In vocational schools we might consider one of the most urgent issues to be a reconstruction of timetables to include regular 'one-to-one' sessions as well as smaller-than-usual groups. Other issues should be the provision of more repertoire classes (with the inclusion of a wider range of styles and choreographers), the raising of standards in these classes (by more attention being given to historical and personal choreographic details), the regular video-recording of students' work (specially in the repertoire classes) and then the teaching of students to assess themselves on video. (The school's video library should be enlarged and made regularly accessible to students.) Dance notation should be made a compulsory subject.

It is also imperative to create an atmosphere in schools where young dancers may become more self-confident and independent, and mentally mature enough to achieve sufficient self-criticism and knowledge about their own talent, looks and technical capability. Most importantly, teachers should keep an open mind and avoid any pre-conceived ideas by putting youngsters' artistic potential in 'pigeonholes'. Students could be advised about their special abilities and their weaker points and helped to find self-identity. Their versatility should be enhanced to the utmost by definition and analysis on how to interpret subtle differences in style followed by a performance given adequately and in good taste.

At a professional level there are also many matters which could and should be changed for the better, amongst the first being the artistically unsatisfactory, short-sighted and often humiliating audition practices.

At open auditions, all choreographers, directors and producers should respect dancers enough to see their class-work in small groups instead of the infamous 'cattle-markets'. They should always give each an opportunity to perform individual, demanding and versatile tasks.

At school-associated companies, artistic directors should rely less on references passed on by the school and should make decisions mainly on the basis of impartial and individual auditions and interviews with the incoming graduates.

From time to time within companies there could be further, voluntary auditions before an artistic panel (which could include guest choreographers and other invited outside experts) for specific roles or for reasons of promotion within the company. At these occasions dancers should feel free to present themselves in their own, individual interpretation of roles (or at least in excerpts) which they would like to perform and for which they have not yet been cast. These auditions could be videotaped and then, for the sake of self-awareness, could be studied and assessed by the dancers themselves, ideally, if possible, together with the panel. To create the right atmosphere for these occasions the dancer and panel members could discuss and argue about the personal inter-pretation. Such discussions may lead to new ideas and should help to develop a constructive and creative relationship between inter-preting artists and the artistic direction.

The alteration of dancers' often insulting circumstances world-wide should start by a change in some attitudes amongst dancers, choreographers and artistic directors, but first of all in those of the teachers! By the nature of our work we are responsible to a greater degree for the mentality of both dancers and dance-makers. If we operate with myopic and despotic attitudes and rely on precon-ceived ideas, we shouldn't be surprised if those dancers whom we have taught in such a manner will behave in similar ways when they reach positions where they are in charge of new dancers' careers and, what's more, they also hold the future progress of the dancing profession in their hands.

Index